Bar Scams Exposed!

How to Spot Thieving Bartenders & Other Tricks of Their Trade

By Alan Mitchell

ISBN: 1480276316
ISBN-13: 9781480276314

This book is dedicated to the late

Andy Levy

He set the bar for Bar Spotting

&

*the late **Alan Kirschenbaum***

Who said to Alan Mitchell:

"This stuff belongs in a book."

About The Author

In 1971, while attending college part time and going to the race track full time, my next door neighbor stopped by and asked if I wanted a part time job for a company that was located next to the lawyers office where she worked. The job was as a part time stock boy, 3 days a week – Monday, Wednesday and Friday's, about 2 – 3 hours a day. My job was to mail back items that were purchased at various locations.

About 2 weeks into the job, I asked my boss what I was doing, where all this crap came from that I was returning. He then explained what they did. He told me they go to retail locations, 4 in a group, and attempt to catch the cashier stealing money from the register. The group of 4 would enter an establishment (they had many drug stores of the day as clients, as well as other retail locations), separately. They would each purchase items and have the exact change to pay for the items. The 4 "operatives" would line up at the register, with their purchases, and attempt to "rapid fire" through the line, paying for items and then quickly moving along. The next operative in line would check to see if the previous sale was rung through. This would make it easy for the cashier to leave the register drawer in the open position between sales as the operatives paid exact change for their items. Most of the time, the cashier would enter the cash from one or two exact change sales directly into the drawer without physically entering the transaction through the register. The company would then bring in a polygraph machine and operator, and they would question the employee on the spot. The company would then be paid a percentage of the amount the cashier admitted to stealing.

Then, as time progressed, I learned that this company also offered another service that they called "bar spotting." Bar spotting was the art of catching bartenders who were attempting to circumvent the system. At the time I was 20 years old, not legally old enough to drink in Philadelphia. When I told them I was 20, they asked if I had any family members who might want to do this. My father and uncle then took part time jobs, and when I reached the age of 21, I started bar spotting, as well.

This was a "different" type of job. Any job where you are required to drink liquor while on duty would be considered a "different" type of job. Imagine, a long haired hippie looking dude, just turned 21, going into the 'most' classy restaurants in Philadelphia and then, in Manhattan. I looked out of place in almost every establishment that I went to. Still, I paid attention to what the boss told me to look for and before long, I started catching bartenders "in the act." In a matter of a few weeks, I spotted bartenders placing cash directly into the tips, or placing cash from sales into their pockets, or the one girl who placed cash from sales down the front of her pants. I also discovered the most prolific infraction, the giving away of drinks to friends and strangers for bigger tips.

I bar spotted for the next couple of years, until I left the industry for greener pastures. Then, after selling another business in 1989 my wife asked "what's next?" I told her I had this one idea – and I told her what that idea was. Of course, she laughed (liked so many others). But I did agree that if the phone did not ring (with customers), that we would figure out something else to do. That was in 1989. The phone still rings.

Alan Mitchell

Sincere Thanks to Those Who Have Helped and Inspired Me Along the Way

Garry A Kramer	Editor-in-Chief
Marsha Mitchell	Inspiration, Brains
Bonnie A Steiner	Proof Reader, Brains
Jeffrey Mitchell	Title Maker, Highly Constructive Criticism
Michael Czyzyk	Bar Spotter Extraordinaire
Thomas LaRossa	Bar Spotter Extraordinaire
Lance Mitchell	Bar Spotter – Still Moon Servant
Julie Mitchell	Librarian Extraordinaire
Brian & Abby Smith	Honest Evaluators
Steven & Donald Mitchell	Introduction to Tito Vodka
Jerry Steiner	Inspiration. Telling Me What I Should Do
Joe Shamy	Brilliant Club Owner & Friend

Readers:

The stories within the covers of this book are from actual Bar Spotter reports. The same reports are submitted to the bar owners of each establishment. The person who does the "bar spotting" and reports is my longtime employee Bartholomew "Bart" Enders. Bart has been Bar Spotting since 1989. He watches bartenders...that's what he does. Bart has 'seen it all' and he is 'The Best' at what he does.

All stories in this book are true – as reported by Bart.

When Bartholomew Enders is Bar Spotting, he is the crooked bartender's worst enemy!

— *Alan Mitchell* – owner ETD Reporting Service

Table of Contents

Table of Contents

Table of Contents

Chapter 1

It Starts at 'The Top'

There is an owner for every bar. Consider him "the Boss." As the boss, he hires people to work for him. When any bar owner hires employees, the job should come with a set of rules and procedures for them to follow. When a bar owner gives the rules to the employees, he expects that the rules will be followed. One way for the boss to check on whether the employees are following the rules is to hire a service that specializes in "spotting" on employees. The "Bar Spotter" is a sort of "Secret Shopper" who specializes in bars and restaurants. The Bar Spotter checks to make sure the rules and procedures of the owner are followed. A successful boss is one who has his employees follow his direction and who is respected and obeyed by them. When employees follow his rules, the owner's liquor costs remain low and they remain happy. When employees don't follow the rules, anything can, and will, happen.

Bartholomew "Bart" F. Enders has been Bar Spotter since 1989. He is the true authority on the subject. He's spotted thousands of bartenders at hundreds of bars along the east coast. He's seen all the bartender's "tricks," some of which are in the stories below. From stuffing register cash into the tip bucket to "giving away the house." You may be surprised at how many variations there are on the same theme.

This book is intended to show the many "tricks" available to bartenders to earn extra money. The owner of the bar then must find ways to combat the bartender's "moves." This can usually be done through enforcing rules and regulations. Bar owners should have a zero tolerance policy when it comes to employee theft.

The stories and instances are from actual Bar Spotter reports. Then, in **BOLD FACE**, Bart critiques the "move." The bar owner then must try to combat that "move." It's a game of "chicken" with very high stakes.

All bartenders are expected to go directly to the register, immediately after each sale, on every occasion and account for those drinks by cash or tab. It sounds easy. However, as the stories below will indicate, it does not always happen. There are numerous ways to exploit this procedure, always in the bartender's favor. Note the many subtle differences in bartenders' styles – all based on the same themes. Remember, many dishonest bartenders are opportunists who go from bar job to bar job, until they get caught.

Who Are These "Crooked" Bartenders??

There are a small percentage of bartenders who would be considered opportunists. They go from bar to bar, exploiting the cash register and system for personal gain. When they get caught, they simply move to another location and setup shop. The unsuspecting bar owner starts by thinking he has a good employee. Then, after a few weeks, he sees erosion in his liquor percentage. That is, the amount he spends on liquor vs. the amount rung via the register. When liquor costs rise, and the amount of cash rung via the register does not rise, well, therein lies the problem. At that point, the light goes on in the owner's head.

What Is A Bar Spotter?

A Bar Spotter is a person (or company), that goes to establishments that have liquor licenses (bars, taverns, nightclubs, hotels, etc…), and reports on the conduct of the employees. It is mostly about watching the bartenders to see how many drinks they give away, how much money they steal, how much liquor they overpour, and how they treat the clientele.

Who Hires A Bar Spotter?

The bar owners who have "the need to know," the accountants who keep their books, as well as those who own multiple establishments. Owners who realize that success starts with strong management, the smart bar owners (ones with low liquor costs), increase profits from the information from the reports. In essence, the reports pay for themselves.

How Often do the Spotters Visit the Locations?

It depends on the situation and owner, but for best results monthly works best. That way days and shifts can rotate as the information keeps coming.

Is The Spotter Always The Same Person?

Not always. For best results rotating spotters' monthly works best.

Should the Owner Tell Employees when the Spotter's are Coming In?

Never. Employees should not be privy to the information in the reports. Only the owner of the establishment should see the reports. The owner is holding "all the cards." Then, the owner can use that information when addressing the bartender. Example:

If the owner has a report that says the bartender gave away six drinks, he can meet with that individual and relay what he wants him to do in that situation in the future (write down on a piece paper that a drink was given away, ring it on a "comp" key on the register, or don't give away those drinks). When the spotter arrives next time, if the bartender continues to do the same thing that he was told not to do, he's "out."

The best results are gained when bartenders are unaware of being watched.

Why Can't The Owners Use Cameras to watch the staff?

They can use surveillance cameras to observe the staff, but there are a couple drawbacks.

First, someone has to monitor the video. This is done in real time. Not many owners watch the cameras with consistency after they install them. Many owners have the spotters in, and then note the times on the reports to identify the problem using the video. Also, watching these videos can be as boring as watching paint dry.

Next, unless a camera is trained on the register display, an owner can only tell if the bartender is going to the register, not what is being rung. If the camera is not trained on the register – it is really worthless.

Chapter 2

Understanding the Bartending Racket

Bartender's View

Bartenders make their money via tips. It's like having their own franchise – generated by the amount of tips they receive. If the bar/club owner does not promote his business properly, the franchises (tips) suffer. When tips suffer, bartenders suffer.

Cause Of Action

For those crooked bartenders who are seeking extra cash while on duty, the object of the exercise is to remain employed at one location as long as possible, until they get caught. Some are performing the "moves" mentioned in Bar Scams Exposed! (a "move" is when the bartender makes an assault on the register). Some moves may be mundane and appear easy (usually less reward); other moves may be more elaborate: Risk versus reward.

Bartending In Its Honest Form

Bartending in its most honest form is when the bartender is polite, approaches the customer, makes a little small talk, takes, prepares and serves the order, then goes to the register to enter the sale. At the register he rings through the total properly, enters the payment and closes the drawer. Most would thank the patron as they return the change. The bartender is then left a tip. If it's a neighborhood bar and he makes his $100 per shift in tips, he's usually happy.

▶ Bart's Assessment:

There are many honest bartenders. Hard workers who follow the rules and do a good job for the boss. Based on the reports over the years, it is estimated that more than 50% of the bartenders observed receive favorable reports (no major infractions). Those honest bartenders will find *"Bar Scams Exposed!"* fascinating. However, it's the other approximate 50% of bartenders that we observe where the trouble occurs for the bar owner. Those 50% will identify with the incidents in this book.

Bartending In Its Dishonest Form

Most of the "really good" crooked bartenders do not try to hit a 'home run' every night. They know eventually it will catch up with them. After a period of time, a light may go off in the owner's head that the liquor costs are high (you would be surprised to know that very few bar owners know their liquor cost number – which is the most important number they should know – if they spend 21% - 23% they are doing well). Those crooked bartenders make their moves when they feel safe. They know when the opportunity to "earn" some extra cash is at hand, and exploit it.

► **Bart's Assessment:**

There are many dishonest bartenders, as well. *"Bar Scams Exposed!"* will examine and critique their every move.

Here's What Some of the Really "Good Ones" Do

The "really good" ones pick a different time period every day. They don't crush the owner at the same time every day. The best time is when the bartender is familiar with most of the patrons at the bar. They have a time period, perhaps 30 minutes (never more) or a set amount they want to make – over and above tips. During this time period they still enter some sales through the register properly. They can't have a half hour of no sales (or No Sales) showing on the register tape. They use different methods such as throwing cash directly into the tips, or charging for one drink via the register when they serve two or three. The cash adds up quickly. At the end of the time period, they STOP! At that point, they have their extra cash. They go about the bar business properly. The bartender then has the remainder of the shift to get the cash out of the register, which can always be done with an exchange of the tips.

Another thing that is very important – if the owner of the bar allows the bartender to reconcile the register at the end of the shift, every move becomes easy. But again, the "smart ones" are careful not to overdo it.

The Daily Routine

Bartenders in taverns and neighborhood bars usually use the $100 **tip mark as a good night**. In night clubs, it could be much more (they have fewer days of the week that are busy). The stories in "Bar Scams Exposed!" will explain how bartenders make extra cash while on duty.

Bartender Styles

The most successful 'thieving' bartenders are the ones who have an air of coolness about them, the ones who can rip off the owners and never show a sign of worry.

However, when many bartenders are making a move on the bar owner (and register), they can't remain calm and collected. They become excited, or nervous, and their demeanor changes. For them, a shorter period of 'thievery' is called for. Maybe only fifteen minutes to start, then possibly increase the time as they feel more comfortable.

First Things First
The Pouring of Liquor

The "smart ones" know that overpouring liquor for no reason is ridiculous. Let's examine this:

Bartender's helping themselves to cash at the register should realize that it will ultimately take a toll on the owner's liquor costs (although it takes some bar owners a long time to figure this out). Overpouring liquor increases that same (liquor) cost. ***Why do it?*** The smart ones don't. If anything, they "underpour" liquor. Therefore, the decreased liquor costs from underpouring drinks can go a long way when helping themself at the register.

Another thing, bartenders that overpour liquor for bigger tips, unless they inform the customers that the drink is overpoured or extra strong, the patron usually won't make the correlation. Overpouring liquor is a total waste. It increases liquor costs for zero gain.

Second Things Second.
The Easy Stuff
All Crooked Bartenders Know

There are many bar owners who allow the staff to place the night's receipts, along with a "Z" (final) total from the register, into a bag at the end of the night, and place it somewhere in their office or in a safe. As mentioned, this creates one of the easiest 'moves' ever!!! Here it is...

Throughout the bartender's shift, they take a certain amount of time, say a half hour, and during that half hour, ring half of all sales via the register (charge all patrons full price), but still deposit all of the cash, from the sale, into the register. At the end of the shift, when the bartender "Z's" out the register ("Z"ing out the register is taking end of the night total), they simply make the total on the register tape match the total in the bag. The rest is theirs. It's not Rocket Science. If the register says they did $700 in business and there is $800 in the register, the extra $100 belongs to the bartender (that was the remainder of the half amounts rung via the register). When they add that $100 to their $100 in actual tips – well, it becomes a very good night. Will the owner miss this amount every night? Not if there is a decent amount left in the register for him. The one caution to using this move is that it is very, very, very easy. Easy to become piggish. If the bartender uses some restraint, this "move" could go on indefinitely. Especially if there is ample business on a daily basis at the bar. Then once the bartender is finished making this move during a given shift, it's over. Tomorrow is another day.

The "Blind Drop"

Bar owners, but especially nightclub owners, sometimes use what we will call a "blind drop." That is, going around to the register an hour or two prior to the shift ending, running "X" totals on the register (an "X" total is the amount rung through the register to that point of time), changing the drawer and counting the cash in the register. It's a smart thing to do! If the owner sees an overage in the drawer at that point, the bartender should have some explaining to do. The smart bartenders respond by saying, "I was trying to expedite drink service so I placed some of the cash in the drawer without totaling it on the register. It was faster." Believe it or not, if that cash is still in the register, the owner usually lets them slide. If that happens, the smart bartenders do not make any moves for another month or two, as the owner will probably be watching.

▶ Bart's Assessment:

If the bartender already took the cash out of the drawer, then the total on the register tape should match the amount of cash. At that point, the bartender is "in the clear." The BIG loser here, as always, is the owner!

Here We Go!!!

Okay. So now it is time to examine actual stories of thievery and treachery from the actual Bar Spotter's reports. All paragraphs appear almost exactly as they were submitted to the bar owners (some names have been changed and some descriptions deleted – but the stories are actual).

The Nightclubs

The next two items below are mind boggling (the second item is entitled "A Better Way to Do It"). It depicts how different bartenders perform the same "trick," only going about it with different technique. One would have to agree that the second story, of the two, shows bartenders who are a bit higher up the bartender evolutionary chain. They are a bit brighter and not as brazen.

In this first item, not just are the bartender's actions heinous, but the owner's response priceless. This bar owner falls into the category of "I have another business which does well, so I bought a night club" (he owns numerous, busy gas stations). Aside from having lots of money, he is among the most clueless bar owners ever encountered after 23 years in the business. Here it is:

On the report, the question is listed as "IS BARTENDER ACCOUNTING FOR ALL SALES PROPERLY?" The answer, on this occasion was, "No."

There were two registers at this bar. When first arriving at the bar, there was a small amount of what appeared to be random cash next to each register. However, as time progressed, it was clear that the bartender Stuart was taking cash for sales and placing that cash into a pile next to the cash register. He also made change for other sales from that pile of cash. At 1:00 A.M., there were three to five bills located next to each register. By the end of the visit, at 3:00 A.M., each register had a large pile of cash next to it (approximately 50 bills next to each register).

And the other bartenders on duty at this bar:

The two other bartenders (Willie and May), also on duty at this bar, were preparing mixed drinks for patrons, and also exchanging the patron's cash payment with cash that was located next to the register (cash they were stealing). This process occurred on approx. 20-22 occasions during the one hour observation of these bartenders.

▶ Bart's Assessment:

Okay. These three bartenders, obviously, were familiar with the situation. The owner was seldom at the bar and these bartenders were "going for it." Unfettered thievery for two hours.

The owner's response was priceless. He said (agreeing with the bartenders) it helped them expedite drink service with the bar being so busy. He also said the bartenders entered all of that cash in the register later when it was not as busy. When the spotter asked if there was a "big punch" on the register tape, near the end of the night, the owner could not understand what that meant (he said they probably entered those sales as smaller sales, later in the night – which is time consuming and makes no sense). He did however, change the rules. Now, no cash from sales is allowed to be outside of the register. The rule now is for the bartenders to go directly to the register immediately after every sale and make the entries, no matter how long it takes. Now, if the bartenders want to steal multiple sales, they will have to do it another way.

Still more incidents from the same nightclub as above:

At 2:38 A.M., Bartender Valerie was working alone at the Side bar. At this time she prepared two chilled shots of Washington Apple and poured them into "rocks" style glasses. The glasses were filled to the brim. The female patron handed Valerie a $5.00 bill. That payment was placed in the pile of cash next to the register and not entered via the register system.

At 2:41 A.M., Valerie prepared three chilled shots of Patron tequila for two female patrons she was familiar with. Valerie then conducted a $5.00 Miller Lite sale for another patron (not with the two females), which was rung through the register. Valerie then returned to the three shots. She and the two females each consume the shots. No cash was exchanged or entered in the register for these 3 shots.

At 2:44 A.M., One of the female patrons mentioned at 2:41 A.M. introduced a male friend to Valerie. They "hi-fived." The patron was then served a Jack Daniels & Coke. This Jack & Coke was not accounted for after service.

At 2:54 A.M., A group of female patrons located on the left side of the bar was served one clear mixed drink and two bottles of Miller Lite. No cash was exchanged or entered in the register for these drinks.

During this visit, Valerie tilted both register displays upward at different times. This made the "Display" less visible to the patrons at the bar.

More of Bart's Assessment:

So, I can understand the 2:38 A.M. and 2:41 A.M. sales. Both involved taking cash and placing it next to the register. However, the sales at 2:44 A.M. and 2:54 A.M. make no sense. Giving away drinks to these characters is "unprofessional." What if they leave the bartender a $2 or $3 tip. How does the bartender profit from that? If you are not going to charge the patrons, it really hurts the liquor cost for the times when you are "making a move." The drink at 2:44 A.M. could have been an extra $6 in the bartender's pocket, and the three drinks at 2:54 A.M. could have been another $15!!

Next is from a different report, from a different location than the ones above – but the theme is the same:

The question asked was, "Have All Sales Been Accounted for Properly?" Obviously, the answer was "no."

Approximately 75% of bartender Jeff's transactions were accounted for via the register system. For the other approximate 25% of his sales, he merely placed the payment on the back counter without ringing the sale through the register. On occasions when he was given a tip at the same time as the payment, he also placed the tip on the back counter, comingling that tip cash with cash from sales.

► Bart's assessment:

All right, so Jeff was not being a pig. 75% of the sales went to the owner and 25% of the sales were for him (three for you, one for me). However, below is a continuation of his exploits. He absolutely crushes his liquor costs by giving away many free drinks. Eventually, a good "bar spotter" will catch him and a bright bar owner will fire him. He will look back as giving away those free drinks as his downfall in the bartending business. Here is some of what he gave away:

At 2:08 A.M., Jeff served a bottle of Miller Lite to a female patron who he appeared familiar with. This bottle of Miller Lite was not accounted for during this time.

At 2:24 A.M., Jeff prepared two shots, both filled to the brim, with Grey Goose. He consumed one of the shots, while a male patron with red hair consumed the other. The patron was then served a Miller Lite. These drinks were not accounted for in any way.

► More of Bart's assessment:

Just running up the liquor cost for no reason. The only gain is to the friend, who is there to spend money anyway.

Chapter 3

A Better Way To Do It

Now, let us examine these next piggish individuals. At least, they had a better system. The question on the report reads: "Is the bartender closing the drawer after every sale?" The answer was "not at all."

During the entire two hour visit, both register drawers were left in the open position between transactions. Bartender Vince would take cash from some sales to the register and pull the drawer open without ringing the sale through the register. This occurred during this hour at 10:04 P.M., 10:11 P.M., 10:17 P.M., 10:20 P.M., 10:27 P.M., 10:30 P.M., 10:35 P.M., 10:41 P.M. 10:45 P.M. and 10:52 P.M. He would then enter the cash from sales into the register drawer. After the patron would walk away, Vince would withdraw cash from the register and enter that cash into the tip bucket.

And the other bartender also on duty at this bar:

Maggie was the only bartender ringing sales on the West register. She would leave the register drawer wide open between sales. Maggie accounted for approximately 50% of the sales she conducted via the register system, during this time. She would serve drinks, take the cash to the register and enter it into the already open cash drawer. Half of the time she made entries via the register and the other half of the time the cash was entered into the drawer, without ringing the sale via the register. After the sale was completed, Maggie would go to the register and withdraw the cash from that sale and enter it directly into the tips.

► Bart's Assessment:

What an amazing bar owner. To allow this to occur, he's really a sport. But here's the thing: his total take for the night was so good, that the numbers themselves covered up the thievery. He really did not suspect a thing. He owns three bars and thinks this is his "best running" place. After reading the reports, he installed surveillance cameras the next week. The next night (until the cameras were installed), the owner sat at the bar so he would not lose any money. The bartenders closed the register drawer every time when the owner was at the bar.

When the owner asked the bartenders about the open drawer, they told him that they leave the drawer open sometimes because it expedites sales.

Bzzzz. No good. Bad answer. The register drawer opens immediately when the total button is pushed. The bartender doesn't have to wait 20 or 30 seconds for the drawer to open. The reason they left the drawer open was to steal money from the owner. Plain and simple. Nothing else. And these guys are professional and proficient. When the spotter returned to this location a few nights later, on a slower weeknight, two of the same three bartenders were on duty. They worked with the drawer closed.

After losing a small fortune to them, the owner finally got wise. After a couple of weeks of working with the drawer closed between sales, the numbers were up so dramatically, the owner fired every bartender who previously worked with the open drawer. The owner won this battle! Kudos!

Chapter 4

One for You, One for Me. Oh, So Sweet!!!

For approximately 50% of the sales that bartender Mike conducted during the last thirty minutes of this visit, he simply took payment and tips, and just tossed this cash next to the register. On all of these occasions, the sales were not rung through the register system, or accounted for in any way (no cash collected, no tab updated). Later, during an exchange of tips, the cash next to the register was incorporated into the tips.

▶ Bart's Assessment:

An amateur. He, too, got fired!!!!!

Chapter 5

Door A, Door B, or Door C

There were three different ways that bartender Sheena was accounting for sales.

A. She would serve patrons and update their tab immediately.

B. She would serve patrons, then walk around and perform a bar function (remove used glasses), then go back and account for the drink (prior to serving the next patron).

C. She would serve patrons, then serve other patrons, then go to the register and account for the multiple sales.

▶ Bart's Assessment:

Where there are no rules, there is chaos. When an owner hires a bartender, it should come with a set of rules and regulations. Rules, so they know when the owner wants the sale accounted for and how they wanted it accounted for. What Sheena was doing here was simple. She was putting herself in a position to make a "score," at the owner's expense, at any time.

Chapter 6

Procedure – Or Lack Thereof

When bartender Bret was attempting to work at an above average/rushed pace, he would take two drink orders at the same time, serve both patrons and take cash from each. If he needed to make change from one of the sales, he would first attempt to do so with the other patron's cash payment that was in his hand. Then, all cash from sales was placed on the counter of the back bar (by the register) and those sales were not rung through the register. This procedure (or lack thereof) occurred when the volume of business was high. Bret started by placing the cash from a sale of a particular liquor next to that bottle (i.e. cash from a Grey Goose mixed drink would be stacked next to the Grey Goose bottle, cash from drinks prepared with Jack Daniels would be stacked next to that bottle). By 1:40 A.M., there was an abundance of cash from sales being (literally) thrown on the back counter, instead of being placed in front of the bottles (or rung through the register system).

► Bart's Assessment:

A smart bartender can always tell the owner he was "rushed" on a busy night. That he was placing the cash in front of the bottles so he could accurately ring the sales through the register later. The bartender would then assure the owner that all cash was eventually placed into the register (which it was not). Most owners will buy that story, especially if it involves times of heavy volume of business.

More from the same place:

At 1:05 A.M., Bret served a Twisted Tea to a female patron that he had been in conversation with and appeared familiar with. This Twisted Tea was not accounted for, via the register system, during this time (no cash collected, no tab updated).

▶ More of Bart's Assessment:

When this owner read the reports, he immediately defended his employees. He had some ridiculous story that all the cash was rung through the register at the end of the night. I asked if he had a "big punch" (entry) via the register at the end of the night. This owner completely understood. After checking the register tape, there was no 'big punch!' That's when the light went on and the owner knew things were bad. These bartenders, if intelligent, could have had an ongoing supply of the owner's cash. All they really had to do was enter that cash into the register using improper totals – or no totals at all (No Sales). In a situation like that, the cash would have been easy to take from the register (and not leave all that cash lying around). The thing is, these bartenders reconciled their own register at the end of the night. They did not have to use the deception of placing the cash in front of the corresponding bottle (talk about stupid bartenders).

Chapter 7

Antics

A t 1:23 A.M., Bartender Butch served a bottle of Miller Lite to a blonde female patron who was located at the middle of the bar. This female was at the bar with another blonde female. Butch appeared to be familiar with these females, based on a brief conversation they had. This bottle of Miller Lite was not accounted for, after service (no cash collected, no tab updated).

At 1:37 A.M., Butch served a bottle of Twisted Tea to the blonde companion of the female mentioned at 1:23 A.M. This bottle of Twisted Tea was not accounted for via the register system (no cash collected, no tab updated).

▶ Bart's Assessment:

Why would a bartender risk his or her job by giving drinks to friends at no charge? Why bother? What's the gain?

Consider this: four friends of the bartenders' are at the bar and each receives three "free" drinks during the course of the night. First, would they do the same if the role was reversed? Secondly, if the bartender is making a 'move' on the register, this just inflates the amount of liquor going across the bar that is not being accounted for. The bartender would be much better off charging the friends, ringing an incorrect total (but give the owner something), and placing

the remainder of their payment into the tips. In this instance, it looks like "small potatoes," but it's not!

A smart owner might have a rule in place already that states if a bartender is caught giving away free drinks to friends – they're fired. It could be a good deterrent against this behavior.

Chapter 8

Cleavage & Confusion – For The Ages

G inger was not always going directly to the register after sales. Throughout this visit, she often was carrying cash in her hand, from multiple (previous) sales. Also, at times, cash from her hand was either placed into her cleavage or the tip container. When Ginger uses this procedure, it is very difficult to determine what she is accounting for when she finally does go to the register. When Ginger uses this procedure, it is extremely confusing.

At approximately 4:10 P.M., Ginger served a replacement Coors Light bottle to a male patron who she appeared to be familiar with. When she served this drink, she had cash in her hand from a previous sale. She did not take any cash from this patron. She then went to the register with the cash from the previous sale and entered that beer sale via the register. She then returned change to that patron. However, the bottle of Coors Light to the male she was familiar with was not accounted for at this time. The patron did place a tip into Ginger's cleavage.

► **Bart's Assessment:**

Ginger gets an A+ for her "Go Go Bar" work ethic. Using her cleavage to add to her confusing procedure makes her

a real keeper (look Ma, no hands)! It would be hard for the bar owner to conduct business without someone like her. An "Asset" to anyone's business. The thing is, Ginger could probably go forever, just using her breasts and her brains. Not being too greedy could prolong her shelf life.

Chapter 9

Everybody Loses

1:00 A.M. – Bartender Edward was acting in a friendly and flirtatious manner towards a group of three female patrons (all in mid-20's). At this time, he prepared three vodka / cranberry drinks and served them to these patrons, one each. At no time was any cash collected or rung through the register for these three drinks. These patrons had zero cash on the bar. When these patrons exited at 1:10 A.M., there were two $1 bill's left as a tip (total).

▶ Bart's Assessment:

Drinks were $6 each at this place. Three drinks = $18. Instead, $2 left as a tip.

OUCH!!!

Chapter 10

Tap Two Times In The Corner To Open

Bartender Teddy was going directly to the register with cash from sales. When at the register, he would "double tap" the black area in the upper left corner of the register. When he did this, the cash drawer opened without the screen changing. Teddy would then exchange the cash from patron's sales with cash from the register – without the sale actually being rung through. This appeared to be done on some occasions when patrons were paying cash for small orders of drinks. Examples:

At 11:52 P.M., Teddy prepared a Beefeater with clear soda mixer. The patron paid with a $20. Teddy used the procedure of tapping the screen twice in the upper left corner and the drawer opened. The cash was entered in the drawer, but the sale was not rung via the register properly.

At 11:55 P.M., Teddy prepared a "tall" Jack Daniels/Coke using a six second count of Jack (two ounces). The patron paid with a $20. Teddy tapped the upper left corner of the register screen and the drawer opened. The cash was entered in the drawer, but the sale was not rung via the register properly.

12:08 A.M., three Jack/Cokes were served. Teddy double tapped the upper left corner of the register and the drawer opened. Teddy entered the cash in the drawer and returned change to the patron. It did not appear that this sale was rung via the register properly.

▶ Bart's Assessment:

Teddy found a flaw in the register's operating system and exploited it. Tap the black area in the upper left of the screen twice and the drawer would open. I would have given this guy a promotion and a raise for figuring this out. Management had no knowledge of this flaw in the operating system. Drinks at this place are expensive, and Teddy was making a killing. Of course, when the managers received the report, Teddy got fired.

Chapter 11

Soda, Anyone?

On the following occasions, bartender Mickey served mixed drinks to patrons. He then informed the patron of the correct price of the drink(s), but he did not always enter that price via the register. Instead, Mickey rang multiples of $3 via the register, the price of a soft drink. Examples:

At 11:49 P.M., Mickey served an Absolut/Red Bull. He collected $8 from the patron as payment. He rang $3 via the register.

At 11:50 P.M., Mickey served two Grey Goose/Red Bulls. He took $20 from the patrons and rang the sale as $6.

At 11:57 P.M., Mickey served a Grey Goose/soda. He collected $9 from the patron and rang $3.00 via register.

At 12:02 A.M., Mickey served three Coke based mixed drinks and 3 shots of Jack Daniels. Mickey told the patrons it was $40. He took the two twenties to the register and entered an $18 sale.

At 12:08 A.M., Mickey served two Grey Goose/Red Bull's. He took a $20 bill to the register, rang a $3 sale, and returned $2 as change to the patrons (charged the patrons $18)..

At the register, Mickey would make change for the patrons while shifting cash in the register to the slot on the extreme left side. While the spotter was not able to determine the amount being shifted each time, Mickey did remove cash from this slot twice and entered it into the tip container (at 12:05 A.M. and again at 12:11 A.M.).

► Bart's Assessment:

Brilliant!!! Mickey goes directly to the register immediately after every sale and makes entries. So if the owner or manager is standing across the room watching, it looks like this guy is accounting for all sales. He is - but not at the correct prices. Obviously, he was beating the crap out of this owner. And, it was less than a half hour that he was spotted. Imagine how much this guy was 'knocking down' during a full shift. Good work if you can find it.

Chapter 12

Hey! Turn That Register Display Upward

The register displays were turned facing an upward position on both registers, making the pricing impossible to see from the seats at the bar.

► Bart's Assessment:

If the patrons (or spotter) can't see the numbers on the display, there is little chance the owner will ever find out. This is free reign for the bartender. If they have a $20 sale and ring in $5, who's the wiser? If the bartender keeps track accurately, he can always remove that extra cash from the register when exchanging tips for larger denomination bills from the register.

Owners, and this is VERY IMPORTANT - some bartenders think leaving extra cash in the drawer, above the register total, will keep you happy. If the owner is smart he should know that excess cash, over and above the register total, means the bartender either lost track of what he's doing, or, by leaving extra cash, you might think a mistake was made in your favor (which is not true). It's an old trick. If it persisted, I would have that bartender observed by the spotter.

Chapter 13

Gordon, The 'Evil Genius'

When Gordon was using the register, the amount of the sale was displayed approximately 25% of the time. On the occasions that the register did not display the price, Gordon would access the register by using the green "Rapid access screen" (pressing his name on green button on the screen). Then Gordon would ring the sale to see the price (using the register as a calculator). He would then inform the patrons of the price and accept their cash. Before completing the transaction on the register, he would cancel it, and then return to the "home screen." He would then ring the sale by entering a four digit number to access a register screen and open the drawer without the price showing.

▶ Bart's Assessment:

Gordon is a smart guy. He has total and complete command and knowledge of the register. Many bartenders don't have this knowledge. Here is what Gordon was doing. It's 'text book' thievery!

At 9:28 P.M., Gordon served a bottle of Corona to a female patron. He was given several $1s and also took change from the bar. He took that cash to the South register area where he placed it with additional cash that was located under a "rocks" glass. After this cash totaled $20, he rang a NO SALE and exchanged the bills on the bar with one $20 bill from the drawer. He then entered that $20 into the tip container.

At 10:16 P.M., Gordon served a $5 mixed drink to a male patron who was seated at the bar. That patron handed Gordon a $5 bill. Gordon took the bill to the register and rang a NO SALE. After the drawer opened, Gordon then took several bills from the drawer and placed them in the "rocks" glass along with a slip of paper that he had written something on. That glass was then placed behind the register display (out of sight). While the drawer was still open, he took more cash out of the drawer and placed it in a second cup with another note. That cup was also placed behind the register.

At 10:30 P.M., two Coronas and two shots of vodka were served to a male/female couple. Gordon immediately updated a tab, then opened the drawer and withdrew four $1 bills and placed them under the "rocks" glass.

► More of Bart's Assessment:

See? I told you. This guy Gordon is not just a really smart bartender, he's an "evil genius" if you own the bar. He keeps meticulous records of how much overage he was creating, and then, like magic, cash is in the "rocks" glass he was keeping behind the register display, with written notes. If a bartender performs this 'move,' he must be smooth. Personally, I think Gordon had too many steps involved in this 'move' and sooner or later, it would be his downfall. After the owner read the report, it was Gordon's downfall. He got fired!

Chapter 14

The Register Display – Still The Bartender's Friend

Bartender Mark was ringing cash sales via the register in a manner that, when change was not required ($5 given for $5 sale), the total of the sale was not displayed on the register. This represented approximately 50% of the sales. Examples:

At 9:56 P.M., Mark served a pitcher of beer to two male patrons that he appeared familiar with. He said to them, "Fives good." No price was displayed on the register display after this sale.

At 10:13 P.M., Mark poured two shots of Grey Goose into a glass with ice, and topped it off with 7-Up. He told the female patron that he was familiar with it was $4.00. No price shown on register display.

Sales that did require change, (patrons tendering a $10 bill for a $5 purchase) were rung in the same manner, yet a sale price was visible on the register display.

Also,

At 10:34 P.M., Mark walked over to the east register and rang a NO SALE. There was no transaction immediately prior. Mark then withdrew cash from the register, placed that cash into the tip container, and then closed the register drawer.

At 10:49 P.M., Mark entered a sale via the register totaling $8.00. The patron paid with a $10 bill. Two $1's were taken from the drawer, as change. Also taken from the drawer, at that time, was a $10 bill. That $10 bill was placed in the tip container and the two $1's from the register were returned to the patron as change.

▶ Bart's Assessment:

Bartender Mark clearly knows the system. He uses the register display to his advantage. His total knowledge of the register system worked well for him. Excellent manipulation and deception. Charging incorrect prices and ringing "No Sales." Cash going here, cash going there. Mark is the quintessential bartender for any owner that wants his business to fail.

Chapter 15 ·

More "No Sales" On The Register – Tricky?

A t 9:35 P.M., bartender Nicky served a beer each to three female patrons on the East side of the bar. He appeared to be familiar with these females. Nicky took cash to the register for these beers. When the register drawer opened, the register display read 0.00. Change was then made from the register.

At 9:39 P.M., Nicky prepared a Captain Morgan's mixed drink and then served it to a male patron. The patron handed Nicky a single bill as payment (denomination not known to spotter). Nicky went to the north register and pressed two keys (he was looking around the bar as he went to the register). The register display did not change and it read 0.00 after the drawer opened. Nicky placed the patron's cash payment in the drawer. Nicky then took a different bill out of the register and walked over to a tip bucket which was located under the south register. He then exchanged the bill in his hand with several bills from the tip bucket. He then returned to the north register and entered some of those bills into that register and returned change to that patron for the Captain Morgan drink.

► Bart's Assessment:

Let's be realistic. If a bartender is taking cash from patrons for drinks, and then ringing a "No Sale" on the register to account for that sale, well, it's always a ballsy move. For Nicky, it would probably have been better to just put the cash directly in the tips. Either way, if any patron, spotter or other employee saw what was going on, it could easily have cost Nicky his job.

Also, if the owner does a "blind drop," ("Xing" the register and exchanging the drawer before the shift is over), Nicky would be dead in the water if the cash was still in the drawer.

Nicky's response when he got caught, "I was busy and expediting sales." He sure was. The owner didn't buy it and Nicky was dismissed from duty. At that point, like many others before, it was Nicky's time to move to another bar and start again.

Chapter 16

The Tip Container – Still The Bartender's Friend

At 2:25 A.M., bartender Jack prepared three shots of Jack Daniels. Two of these shots were consumed by two female patrons and Jack consumed the third shot. Jack then took cash from the females and placed it directly into the tip container. None of these three shots of 'Jack Daniels' were accounted for via the register system, after service.

At 2:29 A.M., Jack served a bottle of Miller Lite to a heavyset male patron he was familiar with. The patron handed cash to Jack and he placed that cash directly into the tip container. This bottle of Miller Lite was not accounted for via the register system. This patron was acting in an intoxicated manner, as well.

At 2:38 A.M., Jack served a drink using an 8 – 9 second count of Sailor Jerry's rum in its preparation (close to 3 ounces) and served it to a male patron. Jack appeared to be familiar with this patron. The patron then handed cash to Jack that was placed directly into the tips. This drink was not accounted for, via the register system, after service.

► Bart's Assessment:

Jack has it going. The ratio during this time was two drinks for him vs. one to two drinks for the owner. If it was a contest,

41

Jack would get extra strong congrats, except for one thing, the three ounces of Sailor Jerry rum that he poured into one drink for the fat guy mentioned at 2:38 A.M. He really did not have to do that. It inflates the liquor cost and could possibly shorten his shelf life in that location.

For the bar owners, at this time of the morning, this is extremely difficult to detect. Unless the owner is at the bar or monitoring it via his camera system, he's beat.

Chapter 17

Commendation!

On three separate occasions during this time, Bartender John went directly to the register after sales, with cash, and rang in a "No Sale." When the drawer opened, he placed the cash in the drawer. During the next sale, he removed the cash from the drawer and placed it into a tip container that was located next to the register.

▶ Bart's Assessment:

John had this going on for most of the three years he was at this bar. Textbook thievery! He was never greedy. A few 'No Sales' here and a few 'No Sales' there. Who's the wiser? He knew the owner seldom, if ever, came in at night. He had very little chance of getting caught. John was a smart bartender who knew his craft. His ability to exploit the register for three years was really brilliant.

Chapter 18
Bringing In The Booze – The Bartenders Friend

B art caught bartenders doing drugs while on duty, not paying attention to duties, overpouring liquor, acting in an unfriendly manner towards patrons, drinking on duty, having sex (see "Reflections" - Chapter 71) and committing a multitude of other infractions. However, this is about the one bartender who actually brought in his own liquor (Popov vodka when the bar used Smirnoff as its "house" vodka). He thought he was a "cool" operator.

On that occasion, the report included bartender Lance's heavy overpouring of Popov vodka – and it still took the bar owner three weeks to figure it out (three weeks after receiving the report, one morning he was in his bar and he saw empty bottles of Popov in the trash can and realized he did not order, or carry, Popov). At that point, the bar owner finally understood the report (three weeks later!). Lance was a brazen bartender and he had a nice run. The owner said that Lance worked there for almost six years and purchased two rental properties during that time (no red flag??).

After this owner fired him, Lance found another bartending job a few miles away. When spotted for two hours a five weeks later, Lance diverted more than $60 to his tips that should have been entered via the register. When Lance got fired this time, he did not re-surface locally as a bartender.

▶ Bart's Assessment:

Bartenders bringing their own liquor to work, and substituting it for the "house" brand, has been going on forever. If I was making this move (and pocketing the cash from the sales of my booze), I would use the same brand that I was substituting (but that's just me). If the "house" was Smirnoff, I would bring in Smirnoff. Therefore, there is less of a chance of getting caught. This dumb ass (eventually) got caught and fired.

Chapter 19

A Wink, A Smile, And Some Meat

There was an older male patron seated at the bar. He had a beer in a frosted mug on the bar when the spotter arrived. He was then served a soup. When finished with the soup, he was served a Cheeseburger. When bartender Chris handed the check to the patron, in the amount of $14 and change, the patron examined it closely. He then said to Chris, "Did you take out for the drink?" Chris winked at the patron and smiled. The patron left Chris $22, including tip, to reconcile his bill. Spotter saw the bill and the drink was not on it. Also, this male was given meat, in a tin container, for his dog (he appeared familiar with the waitress as well as Chris).

▶ Bart's Assessment:

But really, had the patron NOT looked at the check, and examined it closely, he may never have known that he wasn't being charged for the beer in the frosted mug. Chris and the dog were the winners on this deal. The loser – you guessed it – the owner!

Chapter 20

"Look, I Have Pockets"

4:05 P.M. – The spotter entered and took a seat at the bar. He waited five minutes for drink service while bartender Mick was in conversation with a male patron (wearing a blue T-shirt which read "Why Are Your Tits Looking at My Eyes") seated at the other end of the bar. That patron was the only other patron present at the bar. Mick then came over to the spotter and offered drink service. The spotter ordered a bottle of Bud. Mick picked up $3 from the spotter for payment of the beer. In route to the register, Mick folded the $3 in half, and then ran his finger down the crease, again. Mick then placed that $3 into the back pocket of his jeans as he walked past the register and continued his conversation with the male patron at the other end of the bar. This bottle of Bud was not accounted for via the register system.

4:30 P.M. – Mick served another bottle of Bud to the spotter. He repeated the exact same process as mentioned at 4:05 P.M. (exact payment folded in half and placed in back pocket of jeans).

▶ **Bart's Assessment:**

If any bartender thinks he knows all or most of the patrons at the bar and feels comfortable, then this is an easy way for that individual to accumulate cash quickly. No ringing of "No Sales" or incorrect totals, just cash in his pocket.

Chapter 21

More Antics...

At 1:57 A.M., bartender Tammy prepared three mixed drinks and carried them to patrons seated at a nearby table. Tammy did not ring the register before or after the drinks were served. When she returned to the bar a minute or two later, she served other patrons and charged them for their drinks.

At 2:13 A.M., Tammy served a Grey Goose/Sprite mixed drink to a male patron. She appeared familiar with this male. They had a conversation for approximately two minutes. This drink was not accounted for, after service (no cash collected, no tab updated). The patron exited after this drink was finished. He left a $2 tip for Tammy.

► Bart's Assessment:

So, what was the gain here for Tammy? Tips? Is it worth it to lose your job for giving away free drinks, with the gain unknown (they may or may not tip)? It is ridiculous for her to give away these drinks, friends or not. Tammy is a rank amateur and does not deserve to call herself a bartender!! If she had larceny on her mind, and was the only bartender on duty, she could have charged those patrons and just put the cash into the tips (just for those few drinks). However, she is not that far up the evolutionary ladder!

Chapter 22

Bernie Bernie Bernie

At 11:30 P.M., the spotter ordered a Cactus Cooler (similar to a Jagerbomb) shot. Bartender Bernie then charged the spotter $9.50. After the spotter consumed the drink, Bernie refilled the glass with another Cactus Cooler, without the spotter asking for it. The spotter consumed that shot. Bernie did not account for this second shot in any way. Bernie did not inform the spotter of the reason for this free shot.

It continues.....

Throughout this visit, Bernie was in conversation, on and off, with a male patron named Joe. Joe was drinking Amstel and Bernie was taking cash and going to the register every time. At 11:20 P.M., a friend of Joe's arrived to the bar. At this time, Bernie placed two inverted shot glasses, one each, in front of the patrons (representing a free drink for each). Bernie did not account for these two inverted shot glasses during this time.

▶ Bart's Assessment:

Let's face it, this guy Bernie is no genius. Giving away free drinks will get you just as fired as taking the cash for those drinks and pocketing it. It made no sense to give away any of these drinks (especially to the spotter who didn't order it). Bernie was running up liquor costs with no personal gain.

Someone should tell Bernie that's why God invented pockets and tip containers. Bernie can consider this a "lost night." Bernie should find another occupation.

Chapter 23

Beam Me Up, Scotty

At approx. 10:15 P.M., Scotty poured a set of four shots containing Jim Beam and Peach Schnapps for a group of three blonde females and a blonde male. Scotty did not charge the group for this round. He was later observed charging these patrons for bottled beers at the Special price (Miller Lite, $2.00). Scotty appeared familiar with this group.

At approx. 11:45 P.M., Scotty was greeted in a familiar manner by a male/female couple who had just entered the bar. He served them each heavily overpoured portions of Mandarin Absolut. Scotty was not observed accounting for this round in any way. After finishing this round, these two patrons exited and were not seen again. They left a $2 tip.

▸ Bart's Assessment:

Okay, let's first examine Scotty's 10:15 P.M. transaction. Wow!!! Here is a bartender who clearly does not get it. He pours four mixed drinks, each containing two types of liquor, for what? Was he being friendly because the girls were attractive, and he thought he had a chance to get laid? He didn't! What he really did was to pour out almost 8 ounces of liquor with no real monetary gain to him or the owner.

Scotty should be fired – not for giving away the drinks, but for being stupid.

Now, let's look at the 11:45 P.M. giveaway. More proof Scotty should be fired (or at least drummed out of the union). He gave away two, $9 drinks. Scotty received $2 as a tip and the owner got royally screwed. No real gain to either, but the owner was getting screwed no matter what.

Chapter 24

Greedy Bastards

There were approximately seven occasions, during this hour, in which both bartenders were at the register with cash, entering sales at the same time. The first bartender would enter a sale and the drawer would open. At the completion of that sale, he would leave the register drawer in the open position and the other bartender would then enter the cash from his sale. Then he would make entries. However, prior to pressing the total button on the register, the second bartender would press a "void" key, and that sale would be wiped out. The second bartender would then close the drawer after the change was withdrawn.

▶ Bart's Assessment:

This is a case of a "tag team" using the register perfectly, for personal gain. It looks like the sales are being entered, but what was really happening was that the sales were being voided prior to being rung via the register. Nice execution of this very old move. At the end of the shift, these two bartenders counted out the register and took their tips. They really hit the jackpot on this shift. On those seven occasions, when they were both at the register at the same time, the second bartender was entering transactions from multiple drinks that were served, and then voiding the sale. Lots of extra cash for the tips. Nice work if you can find it!!!

Chapter 25

Another Nitwit Bartender

At 10:25 P.M., Bartender Jesse served a 22 ounce Bud Light and a 16 ounce Sam Adams to two male patrons who just took seats at the bar. The total rung through the register for this sale was $5.00 (should have been $9). Jess appeared familiar with these patrons.

At 10:28 P.M., a heavyset male patron seated in the right corner of the bar was served a clear colored mixed drink. No charge. Jess appeared familiar with this male.

At 10:43 P.M., a male companion to the heavyset male patron mentioned at 10:28 P.M. was served a dark colored liquor and cola mixed drink. No charge.

At 10:56 P.M., a 22 ounce Yuengling was served to a female employee who was going off duty. No charge.

At 11:24 P.M., a bottle of Miller Lite was served to a male patron with black hair. No charge.

At 11:41 P.M., a 22 ounce draft was served to a Hispanic male patron. No charge.

▶ **Bart's Assessment:**

Bartender Jesse started out smart. He had a $10 sale and rang $5 of it via the register. However, what he did after that will insure that he gets caught quickly. It was giveaway after giveaway. Inflating beer and liquor costs would be Jesse's

downfall. Still, he was with the company for five years – and the owner was carrying 35% + in liquor costs for most of that time (industry norm is about 21% - 23%). Jesse used the cash he stole to purchase some duplexes. Now, he is a land baron! He is no longer a bartender.

Chapter 26

"It's On Me" "No Sales" - Everything

4:33 P.M., Kristin was in the process of preparing a shot of Jack Daniels when she realized she did not have enough Jack for a complete shot (slightly short of one ounce). At that point, she looked under the bar for a reserve bottle, but did not find one. She then told the patron the "short" shot is "on the house." The patron then ordered a shot of Old Granddad to follow. That shot was rung up properly.

Spotters tab was paid in cash (two $10 bills – including tip). Kristin left this cash on the side of the register for more than ten minutes. Spotter then exited after finishing drink. His cash was still next to the register when he exited (not rung through register).

► Bart's Assessment:

It should be extremely disturbing to a bar owner, when the bartender tells a patron that any type of drink is "on the house" or "on me" (the bartender). No matter how "short" the shot. The drinks are *NEVER* on the bartender – and always on the owner. Kristin was immature. She hadn't figured out her craft yet.

But the owner's response to this was priceless. He said: "I guess she's entitled to make some tip money, too." At that point, I asked him what his liquor costs were running. He had no clue. It's a great thing when the guy you work for is clueless. Kristin did not get reprimanded.

Chapter 27

Where Did It Go?? What Was That??

A t 9:25 P.M., a "regular" patron by the name of Frank was served a 22oz Domestic Draft. Bartender Mindy rang a $3 sale on the right register and placed that cash in that register drawer. She then went to the left register, opened the drawer and gave the patron a $5 bill and two $1's change from that drawer. Mindy then returned to the right register and marked something down on a piece of paper that was next to the register.

▸ Bart's Assessment:

That was peculiar!

Here's more…

At 9:39 P.M., Mindy served a 22oz. draft to a "regular" patron named Scotty. This beer was not accounted for, via the register system, after service.

At 10:49 P.M., Mindy was closing out a Tab. The screen displayed "Service Total $62." She took several different bills from three patrons that were sharing one Tab. She sorted the cash next to the register, while the drawer was open, and deposited an unknown amount of that cash into the drawer (not all of it). After closing the register, she then counted all the cash in the pile, as well as the cash from her tips. This cash was comingled as it was counted. Mindy then rang a NO SALE via the register and exchanged cash from the combined pile with cash from the drawer. The large denomination bills were then placed in the tip container.

► Bart's Further Assessment:

Confusion at its best!

Still more...

Then, at 10:55 P.M., Scotty received a replacement draft. The cash that was given to Mindy as payment went directly into the tips after service.

► Bart's Final Assessment on Mindy:

Mindy was "working it." Giving cash to patrons from the register, giving away drinks, marking down drinks that were given away on a piece of paper, placing cash here and there. Mindy even had some monetary gain. A bartender such as this can elude an owner for a long time and devastate his cost of liquor.

Chapter 28

Obscuring The Vision!!!

Situation:

There is a small cash register lamp, with a "LITE" label on it, situated above the register. The glare from this lamp obscures the digital display on the register from most areas of the bar. The Spotter was unable to observe the totals of the sales on the register display, from his seat.

At approx. 10:30 P.M.; a male patron named Matt purchased a round of drinks for all patrons at the bar. He exclaimed that he was celebrating the finalization of his divorce. Bartender Julie placed inverted shot glasses and small plastic cups on the bar in front of all patrons to represent the drinks. She charged him $33.00 for the round (this was confirmed when the Spotter walked past and observed the register). This initiated the buying of rounds by some of the other patrons during the next 15 minutes, though the subsequent rounds were not purchased for all patrons at the bar (Julie also had other sales between these rounds). Julie would then go to the register and account for multiple sales, all at once. When Julie used this confusing procedure, combined with the register display being obscured by the light, it was impossible to determine if she accounted for all sales properly.

▶ Bart's Assessment:

Brilliant!!! Obscuring the display and capitalizing on it!!! A license to steal. Julie rang through the $33 sale, but as it turns out (after owner examined the register tape), she did not ring through many other sales. With the register display not easily readable, she has the upper hand. The fact that she is not being greedy works to her benefit. This type of fleecing the owner can go on for years.

Chapter 29

Please Tip Me

At each end of the bar were separate couples. One couple was a male/female in their early 40's, who appeared very familiar with bartender Tom (as if best friends). The male patron grew up with Tom (overheard). Both patrons were ordering drinks (beers and vodka drinks, approximately seven in total). Cash was never exchanged with these patrons and no tab was ever updated. These patrons were still at the bar when the spotter exited.

At the other end of the bar were two female patrons, both in their early 30's. One of these patrons was a bartender at the establishment who said she had the night off. She and her friend were also ordering drinks throughout the visit. They were drinking vodka drinks that contained "double shots." They had a total of six drinks (containing a total of twelve shots). No cash was exchanged and no tab updated after service to these females. These patrons were still at the bar when the spotter exited.

► Bart's Assessment:

If the owner of this place is any kind of sharp businessman, he would see that his liquor costs are through the roof. He allowed bartender Tom to work at his bar for 2 years – and

his liquor costs for both years was running 35% - 38% (should be in the low 20% range). Tom made a fortune in tips at the owner's expense. Working for clueless bar owners certainly has its perks for bartenders like Tom.

Chapter 30

Epidemic Proportions (Giveaways & Marriage)

Donna appeared to be familiar with a group of six patrons who were seated along the mirrored wall. She was providing them with excellent drink service and was also in conversation with them, on many occasions. During this time, Donna served four Miller Lite bottles, at different times, to members of the group. On these occasions, Donna stayed in conversation with them after service. Donna did not account for any of the four beers after service.

There was a member of this group who was wearing a hat. Donna served a Miller Lite bottle to him and did not charge him in any immediate manner, after service.

There was another member of the group who was seated with these patrons. This male received a bottle of Bud, and Donna did not account for it, after service. On this occasion, Donna placed this Bud on the bar while in conversation on her cell phone, and then immediately exited the bar area for the next 8-10 minutes.

▶ Bart's Assessment:

Giving away drinks to patrons – at no charge, is an epidemic in the bar business. Everyone does it and some even get caught. The above transgressions by bartender Donna were

slight. A beer here and a beer there. When confronted about giving away the drinks, Donna was smart. She told the owner she was "building a trade." He bought it!!! Not only did the bar owner buy Donna's story, but he started dating her during the time the report was filed. Then, he married her. Donna hated the spotter report, and now that they are married, they haven't used the spotter since.

Chapter 31

The Oldest (And Dumbest)
Trick In The Book!

Jo-Jo left the cash register drawer in the open position through-out this spotter's visit. There were multiple occasions when Jo-Jo would serve drinks to patrons, take their cash and go to the register. When Jo-Jo was at the register, she would enter their cash into the already opened register drawer without making the entries via the system. Therefore, those drinks were not accounted for. Then, Jo-Jo would take a penny, which was located on the right side of the register, and move it to the left side. If Jo-Jo served two drinks in this manner, she would move two pennies to the left side of the register. On one occasion, when she served four drinks and used this procedure, she placed four pennies from the right side of the register to the left side of the register. Then, at 11:50 P.M., during an exchange of tips for larger bills from the register, Jo-Jo first performed that even exchange, and then she counted out $30 extra from the register and placed that cash into her tips. Jo-Jo then removed all pennies from the register.

▶ **Bart's Assessment:**

Old school, immature move. How obvious can you get? If I'm a bar owner or G.M. walk past a register that has pennies

on it – that bartender should be fired on the spot. Even the dumbest of bar owners know this move. If this is the best move you can do, find another job.

Chapter 32

Keep The Change!! (Literally)

During the entire visit, none of the four bartenders on duty were providing coins as change for any cash sales. Instead, they would "round up" to the nearest dollar amount. Example:

At 8:08 P.M., bartender Mike prepared two Hendricks Gin mixed drinks for a patron. He told the patron the price of $17.60. The patron paid with a $20 bill. After ringing the $17.60 sale through the register, the patron was given two, $1 bills as change ($.40 remained in register).

All bartenders were overheard informing patrons that glasses of wine were "$10, $11, $12 or $13" (even amounts) when the register displayed increments of cents.

▶ Bart's Assessment:

This is intricate and creative, and very good! So, let's say a mixed drink is $8.50 including tax. These bartenders were charging the patrons $9, and keeping the extra fifty cents (not putting any change on the bar). That cash would accumulate in the register and get withdrawn at the end of the shift, or when an "X" total is performed, or during an exchange of tips. This was a very busy bar, so these guys had a great night just keeping the coins – not including tips and salary. To figure this out and exploit it, their creativity is to be applauded!

Chapter 33

Shawn Is Stupid!!!

A t 12:37 A.M., Shawn was observed serving three Miller Lites to a group of attractive female patrons seated at his bar. After serving these drinks, Shawn was not observed returning to the register with cash, nor was he observed adding these drinks to any existing tab.

Immediately after serving the three Miller's Lites mentioned at 12:37 A.M., and not accounting for them, he was observed filling another order for four beers consisting of three Miller Lites and one Heineken. These beers were served to a group of four male patrons who were standing near the DJ booth. No cash was collected for these four beers, nor was any tab updated after these beers were served. Shawn appeared familiar with all of the patrons mentioned above.

By 1:15 A.M., all of the above mentioned patrons were gone. No tip was left by any of those patrons.

► Bart's Assessment:

Giveaways. The bartender's worst enemy!
Shawn's gain from giving away seven beers (six Miller's Lites, one Heineken) was zero! The owner's "take" was less than zero!

Dealing In Euros

At approx. 9:50 P.M., a female patron was in conversation with bartender Vincent. It sounded as if she was attempting to settle her tab, but she only had a 20 Euro note. At first, Vincent claimed he could not accept a Euro as payment. Then, after some conversation with the patron, Vincent was overheard exclaiming, in a playful tone, "Hey, it's my tip!" Vincent then placed this 20 Euro among his tips. The patron exited and the four drinks served to her and her companion remained unaccounted for.

► Bart's Assessment:

Vincent's creativity is astounding. Not accepting Euros for the owner, but accepting them for himself. Never considered this move. You can bet the owner of this place did not like it.

Chapter 34

Ecstasy

At approximately 11:00 P.M., a couple (male with glasses, brown hair and beard; female with long brown hair) entered the bar. They were greeted in a friendly manner by Vincent. Vincent prepared a draft Guinness and three, large chilled shots of Patron Tequila for them. Vincent consumed one of the shots of Patron. None of these four drinks were accounted for via the register immediately after service. During his conversation with this couple, Vincent informed them, "I am so fucked up tonight! I mean, I haven't been this messed up since I worked here on New Year's Eve, and I was doing 'ecstasy' and 'mushrooms' that night!" He continued by saying, "I couldn't tell 'what was what' that night, all of the bottles on the bar looked the same to me, all different colors!" The female of the couple joked, "I'm gonna tell your boss!" Vincent replied, "Go ahead, he's the one that gave the stuff to me!"

As Vincent was conversing with that couple, a male patron came to the bar and possibly overheard part of this conversation. This male appeared to be intoxicated. He first ordered "three mushroom teas" after hearing Vincent's testimonial about hallucinogens. He then ordered some drinks that Vincent could not prepare due to his level of intoxication (patron ordered Irish Car Bombs and an Old Fashioned). Vincent convinced the patron to order three vodka Martinis, informing the patron (at that time) that the charge would be $21. Vincent prepared these Martini's very slowly, by chilling the glasses first. Then he served the Martini's to the patron. The patron then attempted to pay with a credit card. Vincent informed him that the payment had to be cash only. The patrons handed Vincent $25 (a twenty and a five). When Vincent completed the sale, the register display read "$11.00." Four, one dollar bills were returned to the patron.

As this same male patron returned to his two female companions who were seated at a table with the drinks, he tripped over the foot of one of the two females and fell in a manner that made a very loud noise. All three "full" Martini glasses had broken. Vincent allowed the two female patrons to clean up the broken glass. He did not come out from behind the bar to assist. They brought pieces of broken glass to the bar, piece by piece, and one of the females requested a bar towel from Vincent. She cleaned the area with the towel, and then placed this towel, with small bits of broken glass adhering to it, on the bar. Vincent then placed this towel in the depression of the bar, to be used again (it should have been placed away from the bar and patrons).

At approx. 11:10 P.M., it appeared that many patrons were exiting the bar. At that time, Vincent was overheard exclaiming loudly, "Hey, I'm gonna buy everybody a round, what do you want?" Approximately seven patrons were ready to exit, wearing coats. They all refused his offer. However, another male patron at the bar overheard the offer. This patron assumed that Vincent meant "everybody" literally, so he said to Vincent, "I hear you're buying everybody a drink, can I order one?" Vincent then informed the patron, "I meant those guys, they've been here since four o'clock." Vincent did not give a free shot to this male.

At one point, a patron asked Vincent for change to use the juke box. The patron walked away from the bar to use the juke box, leaving his drink on the bar. Vincent cleared away his half consumed drink. The patron had to inform Vincent that he left his glass on the bar, and that it was no longer there. Vincent replaced the drink for him at no charge. The patron tipped Vincent $2.

▶ Bart's Assessment:

Vincent probably did some Ecstasy, some Magic Mushrooms, smoked some good Weed, maybe did a little Cocaine or Crack (who knows) and he was definitely 'doped up.' Even in Vincent's intoxicated state, he was still able to net $10 in stolen cash. When the owner of this bar received this report, he called Vincent at home and fired him "on the spot."

Chapter 35

"Hi-Fives" = Loser, Loser

11:35 P.M., A group of four male patrons entered and all approached the bar together. They were familiar with bartender Tony and Tony was clearly familiar with them. As they approached the bar, each of these males "hi-fived" Tony and one of the males "hi-fived" with him a second time. Each of these males ordered a bottle of Corona. Tony did not account for these four Corona's after service.

11:50 P.M., Tony served another round of Corona's to the four male patrons mentioned at 11:35 P.M. None of these Corona's were account for after service.

12:10 A.M., Tony served another round of Corona's to the four male patrons mentioned at 11:35 P.M. and 11:50 P.M. None of these Corona's were accounted for after service.

12:20 A.M., Two of the four males mentioned above met two females at the bar. They told the other two males that they were leaving. These two males left zero tip for Tony.

12:25 A.M., The other two males mentioned above left the bar. They left a zero tip for Tony.

▶ Bart's Assessment:

Tony should be ashamed of himself. First off, the "hi-fives" were too visual and the owner saw it. Then, he gave away twelve Corona's to these guys. What was he thinking? The

owner received zero for the twelve Coronas. Then, the patrons exited and didn't tip Tony. He received zero for the twelve Coronas. Tony really does not understand the bartending business, the science of it. He was fired immediately after his shift (before the spotter report was submitted). When an owner sees the "hi-fives," his attention should be aroused.

Chapter 36

Mentally Unstable

For ninety minutes of this visit, there were six patrons at the bar, including the spotter. Bartender Mick served sixteen bottles of beer, in total, during that time. Mick did not account for any of those beers immediately after service. On these occasions, Mick was keeping "Mental Tabs." That is, keeping track of the drinks served in his head, until the patrons were ready to exit, and then inform them of the total. When Mick used this procedure, he sometimes forgot the number of drinks served to the patrons and had to ask. Example:

Two of the six patrons seated at the bar were served a total of six bottles of beer during this time, and they were at the bar, each with a beer when the spotter arrived (they had at least eight beers). When they were ready to exit, they told Mick they were ready to pay. Mick looked up and down the bar, before saying to them, "What did you have?" One of the males said "four Buds." Mick said, "$16." The males gave Mick a $20 bill and quickly exited. Mick then went to the register and rang a $12 sale. He then placed the remaining $8 into his tips.

▶ Bart's Assessment:

This has to drive every bar owner crazy. Mick is just a lazy ass bartender. Period. He brings zero to the table.

There were winners and losers in this one example:

The winners were Mick, who gained $8 on this transaction ($4 on register ring, and $4 tip); and the patrons, who lied to Mick about the number of Bud's they had. If they only had the eight Buds the spotter observed (two upon arrival, served six more), it would have been $32, and then a tip.

The loser, of course, is the owner. At least eight bottles of Bud were served to these two guys and the owners take was $12. Not worth being in business for that!!

Chapter 37

Again, Giving Away The House –
To Zero Gain

9:40 P.M. – Bartender Manny served an Amstel Light to a male patron, wearing a red coat, who was seated at the corner of the bar, near the entrance. Manny said "cheers" to the patron as he served this beer to him. The patron placed cash on the bar which Manny did not touch. No record of this sale made at this time.

9:55 P.M. -- Manny served a Guinness to a male patron wearing large framed black eyeglasses. This beer was not accounted for, after service.

10:00 P.M. -- Manny served a shot of Johnny Walker Black to a patron who was among the group of patrons who appeared familiar with him (five males and three females), at the end of the bar. Manny does not return to the register after serving this shot and it was not accounted for.

10:30 P.M. -- Manny served a shot of Jameson to a male patron seated at the end of the bar who he appeared very familiar with. Manny immediately starts serving other patrons after this shot was served. Nothing was entered through the register at this time for this shot of Jameson.

10:32 P.M. - Manny served a Heineken and another shot of Johnny Walker Black to the male patron mentioned at 10:00 P.M. No record of this transaction is made at this time.

10:45 P.M. -- Manny served a shot of Wild Turkey to a male patron who is among the familiar group at end of the bar (mentioned at 10:00 P.M. Nothing was entered through the register at this time.

11:10 P.M. – Manny served an Amstel Light to the patron mentioned at 9:40 P.M. This patron still had cash on the bar. At this time, Manny walked away after service to wait on other patrons and this drink was not accounted for.

11:28 P.M. -- Manny served white wine to older female patron who is among his group of acquaintances at the end of the bar. No sales transactions made at this time.

The group of eight patrons, who were at the end of the bar, were still present and drinking when spotter exited.

▶ Bart's Assessment:

Manny subtly gave away nine drinks in this two hour period (that would be 27 drinks in six hours) and so far, his personal gain is zero. What was he thinking? Regardless how much they leave him for a tip, it won't be enough. Manny is inflating the liquor number and is on track to get fired. Manny has no clue about bartending. He should find another line of work.

Chapter 38

More Mental Business

Spotter ordered a beer upon arrival. Bartender Mark did not immediately enter the order via the register. He continued to keep a "mental tab" (keeping track of drinks served to patrons in his head) for the Spotter, as well as with several other patrons. Spotter was not given a receipt until the very end of the visit. The drinks on the bill were accurate, and properly charged.

▶ Bart's Assessment:

Some bartender's keep "Mental Tabs" correctly. Still, as a bar owner, are you paying the bartender to be an accountant? No. His job is to serve drinks and account for them immediately after service. Not to try and remember, an hour later, what the patron had.

Chapter 39

Smile – You're On Candid Camera

11:22 P.M., Bartender Mike is at the register, ringing in a sale for multiple drinks (spotter is seated directly next to register). Bartender Jolly steps up behind Mike and has cash from a sale in his hand. Jolly then says to Mike, while the drawer is still in the open position, "You think 'he's' watching?" Mike responded, "I don't think 'he' ever watches." Jolly then entered the cash from his sale into the already opened register drawer – without ringing the sale via the register system.

▶ Bart's Assessment:

Many bar owners have camera surveillance systems installed, as a deterrent to bartender theft. Trouble is, very few owners ever watch them (in the past, bar owners have hired the bar spotter to watch these tapes – which, as I said earlier, is similar to watching paint dry).

However, Mike and Jolly were not so lucky. The owner *WAS* in the office watching and saw the whole thing. Unbelievable!! Both bartenders were fired at the end of their shift.

That was a good gamble gone bad for those two bartenders!

Chapter 40

First I Look At The Purse

While ringing the spotter's Rum and Coke at 8:02 P.M., and a male patron's draft beer sale at 8:04 P.M., bartender Jackie rang the sale via the register system and then exchanged the cash that was given to her by the patron with several bills from the register. She then placed an unknown amount of cash from the register into her purse that was hanging from Ship's Wheel behind bar. She then placed the proper change in front of spotter and the other patron.

► Bart's Assessment:

We've seen cash placed everywhere. Cleavage, bras, next to register, pants pockets – and now a purse. It was a gutsy move by Jackie. Going into the purse for anything would be frowned upon, if the owner saw it or knew about it.

Chapter 41

Quick Thinking

A female patron named Jill was served three bottles of Ultra during this hour (12:02 A.M., 12:23 A.M. & 12:51 A.M.). Bartender Johnny did not charge her for these beers. Johnny appeared familiar with Jill. When Jill exited at 1:05 A.M., she left a $2 tip on the bar.

At 12:21 A.M., and again at 12:53 A.M., Johnny gave a draft beer to a patron everyone called "Fin." Johnny did not account for either of these two beers after service. When Fin exited the bar with Jill at 1:05 A.M., he left zero cash on the bar as a tip.

At 1:35 A.M., an older male patron said, "I want to buy my friend a beer, then the rest is yours," as he was pointing to the pile of cash in front of him. Bartender Johnny placed an inverted shot glass on the bar in front of the friend. The friend immediately said, "I'll take that now." Johnny poured a beer, then removed the shot glass and cash. He thanked the patron and placed all the cash in the tip bucket.

▶ Bart's Assessment:

Bartender Johnny was facing a crisis. He was giving away drinks, thinking his friends would "take care of him" (with tips). They did not. So he did the next best thing. When the easy opportunity arose, he pocketed the cash from the 1:35 A.M. transaction with great ease. It appeared to be approxi-

mately $12 - $15 dollars. He was not being greedy, but he felt he had to make some extra cash. Otherwise, his night may have been a bust.

Chapter 42

Two For You And One For Me

At 11:09 P.M., Bartender Joanie prepared two mixed drinks for a group of three patrons in the northwest corner of the bar. She went directly to the register with the cash from the sale. As she was making change for the two mixed drinks from the register (register drawer open) the third patron in the group asked for a bottle of Yuengling. Joanie then said, "It's $5.50 more." The patron pointed to the change she was holding, as if to say take it out of there. With the drawer open, she entered cash from her hand for the bottle of Yuengling, and closed the drawer. She then returned change for the first two drinks. When Joanie entered the cash for the bottle of Yuengling into the open register drawer, she did not make any entries via the register. That bottle of Yuengling was not accounted for.

At 11:42 P.M., Joanie served a bottle of Corona to a muscular male patron with dark hair. She then took cash from him, rang a "Cash Transfer 0.00" via the register and entered his cash into the drawer. A tip was then given to her and it was stuffed in her bra.

▶ Bart's Assessment:

For the 11:09 P.M. transaction, Joanie had the opportunity and seized the moment. While the spotter did not see her

withdraw that $5.50 from the register (for the Yuengling), you can bet she did!

For the 11:42 P.M. transaction, this was a particularly easy score and she recognized it. Nobody around except for a few familiar patrons (and the spotter). Subtly making money for herself, without overdoing it, Joanie should have a long shelf life in the bartending game.

Chapter 43

According To The (Text) Book!!

A t 7:38 P.M., the spotter received a replacement "rum and coke." Prior to ordering the drink, he placed one $5 and two, $1's on the bar. After the drink was served, Burt picked up the cash and said, "Thank you, boss." He then took the cash and placed it on the back bar between the register and the Service bar. This sale was not rung through the register at this time.

At 7:41 P.M., a couple sat at the bar as they awaited a table in the restaurant. The patron placed several bills on the bar before ordering a "Gin and tonic" and a "club soda." The patron said "Keep it" (the change) as the drinks were served. Burt left the cash on the bar until the couple left the bar area moments later. When cleaning the bar, the cash was put in the same spot as the spotters, next to the register. This Gin/Tonic was not rung via the register.

There was other cash in that location, between the register and the Service Bar, when the spotter arrived at the bar. In addition, there were also approximately three tips he received that were also placed there.

At 7:46 P.M., Burt was observed taking all the cash next to the register and counting it. He then pressed the large metal button on the right side of the register drawer, and it popped open. The cash was then placed in the register drawer and two, $20 bills were taken and placed in the tip bucket.

▶ Bart's Assessment:

Textbook thievery! Keeping cash from sales, comingled with tips, on the side of the register, until it reaches a certain amount – and then exchanging that cash for larger bills. Not original, but brilliant!!

Chapter 44

Shift Drink

Situation:

B ar owner of a popular NYC bar/eatery calls the spotter and says his liquor costs are "through the roof." He said it was as if "bottles of Jameson were walking out the door." He asked the spotter to visit. The spotter filed the following report:

The bartender accounted for all drinks, during this time, via the register system, always immediately after service. However, at 1:55 A.M. (five minutes prior to closing), all members of the staff gathered in the area of the Service Bar. There were eleven employees, including the kitchen help. The bartender poured ten shots of Jameson and one shot of Jack Daniels. All eleven employees toasted glasses and each consumed their shots. Immediately after consuming the shots, a few of the staff members walked away. Others stayed near the bar. The bartender then poured seven additional shots of Jameson and served them to the staff members who were still present. None of these shift drinks were accounted for via the register system.

▶ Bart's Assessment:

When told that the bartender accounted for every sale via the register, and the only giveaways was the shift drink to

99

the staff at the end of the night, the owner immediately responded "I let them have a shift drink, it's no big deal. Keeps 'em happy." The spotter then told him 18 shift drinks, times seven days a week = 126 "shift drinks." That's more than four bottles of liquor a week. The owner's response was priceless. He said, "I never did the arithmetic." He then stopped the shift drink, permanently. That move left him with zero happy employees.

However, what the owner could have done was to offer one domestic beer as a shift drink. It's much cheaper and makes the employees feel welcome and important (as if he cares about them).

Chapter 45
The Look Of Impropriety

There were two male patrons seated to the left of the spotter. They arrived to the bar shortly after 4:00 P.M. One was drinking Gin/tonic (he had 3) and the other was drinking beer (he had 3). They were also eating pizza. However, bartender Todd never went to the register to account for these drinks, after service (no tab updated). At 5:15 P.M., the patrons told Todd they wanted to settle their bill. Todd announced the price of their sale as "$41" from memory (did not go to register to check on total). The patron then paid Todd. He proceeded to the register and entered a sale of $30.54. While the cash register drawer was in the open position from this sale, Todd entered cash into the tip container and also withdrew change from the register. Todd then closed the register drawer and returned change to the patrons.

▶ Bart's Assessment:

A bartender should NEVER exchange cash into the tips from the register while the register drawer is open during a sale. NEVER. If I'm a bar owner, this should be among the worst things a bartender can do. It's like rubbing the owner's nose in it.

Bartender Todd already mischarged the patron. He made $10 plus the tip. But to then call attention to himself by exchanging the cash he just stole, and entering it into the tips at that immediate time takes a lot of guts by Todd.

Other bartenders have to look at it this way: If the owner is across the room and observes this maneuver, he has to say: "What was that? Where did that cash come from?" Todd got caught, due to his spotter's report, and was relieved of duty the next day.

Chapter 46

Here, There And Everywhere

From 12:04 A.M. - 12:09 A.M., bartender Christy counted a large amount of cash from the tip container on the West side of the bar. She still had cash in her hand when the male bouncer that carded the spotter came over with one bill, for change. He handed the bill to Christy. She took that bill (plus all the cash in her hand) and went to the East side of the bar. There, she pulled out a register drawer from under the bar. She exchanged the single bill with an unknown number of bills from that drawer. On the way back to the West side of the bar, all cash (tips and change) were in same hand. She then gave five bills to the bouncer (who delivered them to the Side bar).

When back at the tip container, Christy continued to remove tips from the bucket and stack them in her hand. With a stack of tips approximately three inches thick, she rang a "No Sale" on the west register. The drawer opened and Christy exchanged the tip cash with cash from the drawer. The drawer was then closed and the cash from the register was placed in the tip bucket.

▶ Bart's Assessment:

Whatever that was, it should not be allowed! Carrying cash around the bar and then comingling that cash with other cash from a different register drawer, then going back to the

original register, ringing a No Sale, and entering cash into the tips. Not sure if she was actually stealing anything, but to make change of a single bill (even if it's $100), should not be that difficult.

Chapter 47

Foua! Ya Got Me All Foua!

When Bart answered the phone, the voice identified himself as Jerry Lowe. He was the G.M. for a popular casino. Jerry had a thick New Yorker accent and a very gruff sounding voice. He first made small talk with Bart, asking about what the spotters do and how he would receive the reports. Jerry hired Bart. Jerry explained the following to Bart:

"We have a bar that is not physically on the casino property," Jerry told Bart, "It's across the street. Employees from the casino can go there and drink after work" (at the time, if the bar was not on the property of the casino, employees can drink there. If the bar was on the property, employees can't drink there). Jerry thought his casino employees were going there after work and drinking for free. That was one reason he sent Bart in to "spot" the situation. The other reason was the casino was about to close this bar for the winter season and, according to Jerry Lowe, they wanted to fire the staff instead of giving them unemployment compensation.

Jerry continues, "We have 4 employees working there. A waiter, a busboy, a bartender and a cook. There's no guarantee anything will be going on, but we'll try it and see what happens." The time and location were confirmed.

Bart arrives to the job the next night. The scene was calm. Four employees were present. There was one patron and Bart at the bar. Nothing happening – until now:

It was 1:15 A.M. Since Bart arrived, the 4 employees were really doing nothing except watching the TV in the bar, and bullshitting with each other. At this point of time, the barback steps behind the bar and takes a large sized, white Styrofoam coffee cup out from under the bar. He then walks over to the back bar where the top shelf bottles of liquor are located. He takes a bottle of Johnny Walker Blue from the top shelf, and pours it into the cup, filling the cup more than half way.

The busboy who poured the liquor now places the cup on the bar, where it sits for a few moments. During this time, the bartender was standing with his arms crossed, watching as the busboy places the drink on the bar.

The drink is on the bar for a couple of minutes. The report read: "The waiter picked up the drink from the bar without a receipt, and without it being accounted for. He then took that drink to the service window at the kitchen."

The drink remains at the kitchen service window for another minute. At that point, the chef comes over, picks up the cup, and takes a couple of sips. He then walks away with the cup.

Bart files the report the next day and submitted it to Jerry Lowe, the G.M.

Jerry Lowe read the reports and told Bart, "The bartender allowing someone else to prepare a drink is against the rules. The barback who served the drink was not allowed to prepare drinks. The waiter, delivering a drink that hasn't been accounted for, performed a definite 'No-No,' and the Chef was drinking on duty."

Jerry Lowe, after reading the report exclaimed (in his think NY accent), "Foua, foua, foua. You got me all foua! Bart, you're the best!"

▶ Bart's Assessment:

All "foua" were fired. Justice was served!

Chapter 48

"Don't Worry About That One"

At 6:49 P.M., Bartender Ray prepared a Johnny Walker Black "on the rocks" for a patron who was among a group of three. Ray "free-poured" the Johnny Black by filling the "rocks" glass to the brim, including ice. He also served a second shot of Crown Royal to the patron's companion. Cash was taken from one of the patrons (Johnny Black) and a sale of $8.56 was rung on the register. When the male patron questioned the charge, Ray told him, "Don't worry about that one – pointing to the Crown Royal."

► Bart's Assessment:

One of the guys (Crown Royal) in the group of three was the owner's brother-in-law. Ray had no idea. He was fired after his shift. His gain was less than zero. Not everything goes according to plan.

Chapter 49

The Outdoor Bars

Bartenders who are lucky enough to work in a busy, outdoor environment have this to remember - very few outdoor bars on the east coast have camera systems installed outside. Mostly, they rely on their managers to run the operations. Many managers don't pay attention to the bartenders. Therefore, outdoor bars are usually "free for all" events for the bartenders making a "move." Here it is:

When no management is present, or when management is at its weakest, pick out a specific time period, say thirty minutes of busy bar time, and during that time period, 'share' the proceeds with the owner. A "one or two for you, one for him" ratio sounds fair during this time period. Use a "tip exchange" to remove the extra cash from the register. The added thirty minutes of cash will greatly increase the tips for that day. After the specified time - **STOP DOING IT** (until the next time - but not the same day). Outdoor Bars are lots of fun for bartenders with experience, looking for an easy score. The veterans know the keys to longevity: 1. Do not be greedy, and 2. Perform the remainder of your duties to the best of your ability (every sale rung properly with efficient service).

▶ **Bart's assessment:**

Bartenders: If you are working an outdoor bar, don't be greedy, know your surroundings, and you may never get caught!!

Chapter 50

Teamwork

Situation:

During this time, all seats were in use and patrons were standing one "deep" at almost all areas of the bar. The tables to the north and south of the bar were occupied. The band was performing a "set." Bartender Mike was preparing drinks for patrons in the southeast corner of the bar.

The report read as follows:

On four occasions during this time, Mike used the register as a calculator. This took place at 10:36 P.M., 10:49 P.M., 10:52 P.M., and 10:54 P.M. On all four of these occasions, after Mike used the register as a calculator, the female bartender, also working at this register came over to enter a sale, thereby changing Mike's calculator screen. Then, after Mike served the drinks and collected the cash for the sale, he went back to his screen and realized it had been cleared. He then re-rang the sale via the register in a manner in which no numerical total was displayed. Mike then deposited a portion of the cash into the tip container and the remaining cash was then placed in the register drawer. There were other occasions when Mike used the register as a calculator, and then entered the sale with the numerical display showing a total (appearing to be entered properly).

▸ Bart's assessment:

Fake left and throw right. Fake right and throw left. It looked like bartender Mike was ringing sales through correctly, and getting the correct total for the patron by using the register as a calculator. However, he figured a way to circumvent the system. That's right, the old "void" one sale and replace it with something that nobody can see.

Be aware that when Mike entered the cash into the tips, he almost had to do that. This bar has many management employees always stalking around. Still, Mike figured it out.

Chapter 51

Confusion Reigns

I t was raining heavily and the register was out of use (covered with green trash bag) on the east side of the Tiki Bar. Bartender Joanne and the other bartender on duty, Shannon, were marking down their sales on a white pad that was located next to the register, where they kept the cash from those sales. It appeared that Shannon was doing most of the writing (Joanne would tell her what she served and she would write it down on a white pad). There were many sales that appeared to be marked down on the pad. When spotter purchased an OJ (no liquor), he paid Joanne. She took that $2 and placed it next to the white pad without mentioning it to Shannon. This sale for OJ was not marked onto the pad next to the register.

8:31 P.M., a male manager (bald) went behind the bar and started to tinker with the cash register. He unplugged it and then plugged it in again. After a few minutes, he walked away. However, the trash bag was still covering the register, which was not being used. Cash continued to pile up next to the register.

8:37 P.M., the manager returned, went behind the bar and started working on the register again. He lifted the trash bag half way up, over the screen. At this point, and through the remainder of the visit, the screen was half blue and half gray.

8:40 P.M., the manager who was fixing the register walked away. The bartenders have been marking drinks to the pad, located to the right of the register. They were also placing cash from sales in that area. At this point of time, Joanne went to the register and started entering some of the cash into it. She used a key on the bottom of the bottom drawer, to open that drawer. At the same time as she was performing those sales, she was also entering cash into the tips (cash next to the pad – where the spotter's $2 went for his OJ purchased from Shannon). This entire process was very confusing.

▶ Bart's Assessment:

With all that cash next to the register in plain view, the manager should NEVER have walked away until he observed that it was all entered via the register properly. Like at any Tiki Bar, the season is short. For the owner to lose cash from those sales, due to the manager walking away is inexcusable. The spotter estimates there was close to $200 next to the register from sales. In excess of $80 of it went into the tips (at least four $20's plus other smaller bills). Good help is hard to find!

Chapter 52

I'll Kick Your Ass!

A Bar owner named Dante called the office on a hot, late July Friday afternoon. Dante explained that he and his brother Nick recently purchased a nightclub "downa shore." Dante quickly added, "it's a short season." Dante then explained that they had a bartender they hired a few weeks prior named Colin. Dante said Colin's register, shift after shift, was "cock-eyed." Dante asked if the spotter could come in the next night, a Saturday, to watch Colin. The response was, "Yes."

Bart arrived and he knew his assignment. He knew what bartender Colin looked like and the register he was working (Dante told Bart that Colin looked like white bread with mayo, with reddish hair – think a youthful looking Conan O'Brien). Bart entered and found Colin instantly. He then went to a seat with a clear view of the register. Bart orders a beer from Colin as he settles in to observe the activities.

Colin's conduct was amazing. A total pig. He was sweating and looking around suspiciously when he had cash from sales in his hand.

There is was! For every 10 drinks Colin served, 3 – 4 were accounted for via the register properly. The cash from the remainder of his sales were going directly into his tip container, which was a large sized champagne bucket directly next to the register. The cash from the sales he was not ringing filled the tip bucket quickly. Midway through the visit the tip container was overflowing with cash. Colin used his fist to mash the bills down in the bucket. There was more cash entered into the tip bucket, as compared to the register, "by a lot."

Bart observes that Colin was stealing money and the tip container was overflowing. Bart continued to observe Colin.

After a few more minutes, Bart stepped outside to call Dante. Bart told Dante about Colin's thievery. Bart told Dante to meet him in the parking lot in a few minutes, which he did.

What followed was unbelievable:

Bart and Dante met in the lot. Dante was fuming mad over this situation. Dante was not only mad at Colin for ripping him off, but he was really pissed off at his brother Nick for hiring this guy in the first place.

Within one minute of meeting, Dante phoned Nick and told him to come outside to the lot. Nick steps out to the lot and Dante introduced him to Bart. Bart then brought Nick up to date about Colin putting cash from sales into the tips.

Dante then says to Nick in a belligerent way, "What the fuck did you hire this guy for? I told you he was a bum. He was unemployed without an excuse and you hired him anyway, you fuckin idiot." Nick fires back, "I do the hiring. If you want to do the hiring - you do it, you jerk off."

The war of words escalated between the brothers. During this time, Colin was still behind the bar robbing them blind. Then, after about 20 seconds of loudly arguing, Dante made a fist with his right hand and he hit Nick across the side of his head and ear. Hard. They started to fight on the lot, all out.

Both brothers were dressed for work, and each was wearing a nice pair of black dress slacks. Dante wore a blue button down shirt and Nick had a patterned silk shirt. Within a minute, each of the brothers were rolling on the ground, in the parking lot, cursing at each other and fighting. After a minute of rolling and fighting, each sustained cuts, Dante on his face and Nick on his arm, under his ripped shirt.

Bart finally got the brothers to stop fighting by telling them that Colin was still in there, behind the bar, ripping them off. Dante said to Nick after they cooled down, "Get that fucker out of there, now!" Nick says, "We got no one to replace him at this minute."

Dante then told Nick to "Sit at the fucking bar, for the rest of the fucking night and watch him, so this fuckin asshole doesn't rip us off anymore. And after the shift, fire him."

Nick responded, "Fire him? I'll kill the mother fucker first." Nick further asked aloud, "Do I cut him up and place his body parts in the bay? Or, do I just cut off his fuckin balls and feed them to the seagulls?"

Bart told the brothers they won't lose any money tonight because of this guy. Neither of them understood. Bart said, "at the end of the shift, just confiscate his tip container, which is holding all the cash he stole, and add that cash to the register. No killing anybody. No cutting off any balls. Just a firing."

Back in the bar, Nick, still disheveled and very mad took a seat at the bar. Bart was 3 seats away, observing. Colin sees Nick taking a seat at the bar. Colin's pale white complexion just got whiter. Colin sensed something bad was going on, and he knew Nick's reputation as a hothead. Bart was enjoying the scene.

Colin could not concentrate on his job with Nick seated at the bar, blatantly watching him and looking at the filled tip bucket. Nick then says to Colin, "Look at those fuckin tips, the bucket's filled and it's only 1:20." Colin replies, "It's been busy, lots of tips." He then goes to wait on customers, but still "shitting his pants" over the situation. Nick stared coldly at Colin as he prepared drinks and Colin felt the dagger-like stare. Nick's face still had a bit of blood from a cut he sustained in the fight with Dante, and his shirt sleeve is noticeably ripped.

A few minutes went by. Nick was watching Colin go directly to the register and account for every sale (with Nick seated at the bar,

Colin wasn't about to do anything crazy). Then, Nick said to Colin, "For the last few minutes, I didn't see you put one nickel in the fucking tip bucket and it's been busy. I thought you said you were getting a lot of tips." Colin had no response, but he was sweating.

Colin then took orders from some customers at the far end of the bar from where Nick was seated. In the process of taking the order, a barback, Mike, was nearby refilling the beer cooler. Colin says to Mike, "Hey man, can you watch the bar for a minute? I have to go to the bathroom." Mike said sure. Colin tells Mike he'll be right back.

Colin then exited from behind the bar. Nick sees Colin exit from the bar and go in the direction of the bathroom. At that point, Nick loses sight of Colin. However, near the bathroom was an Emergency Exit. When Colin got near the bathroom, he bolted out of the Emergency Exit, never to be seen again.

Back in the club, Nick loudly appoints Mike, who is inexperienced, slow and unsure behind the bar, as the new bartender for the rest of the shift.

▶ Bart's Assessment:

These two brothers should never have been in the bar business to begin with. This was their only summer in the bar business. By the next summer – they were gone!

Chapter 53

Other Bar Room Musings

Because It's Not Always
About Stealing!

At a very popular Tiki Bar, early summer - late afternoon, bar owner Charlie hired Bart to spot some bartenders for him. Bart had previously worked for Charlie and knew he liked to drink at his bar. Bart specifically said to Charlie, "*DO NOT HANG OUT AT THE BAR WHEN I'M THERE*." Bart couldn't emphasize it enough. "*If you do, we won't get accurate results*." Charlie agreed that would "definitely" not be there.

The spotter arrived and it was a glorious afternoon. Great weather, beautiful people, and an outstanding band playing Rock N Roll "cover" songs. The band had the crowd singing along and some people were dancing.

The spotter started observing the bartenders on duty. After everything was going okay for a while, the spotter looked around the bar and who is standing there? Charlie. And he was looking drunk. This was just a couple hours after Charlie said he would not be at the bar. The spotter decided to just do his job - stay until the spot is over and then write the reports.

Not five minutes later, with the band playing a cover of Neil Diamond's "Sweet Caroline" and the crowd singing along, improvising the words at different times *("Ho Ho Ho," "So good... So good... So good...")*, drunken Charlie must have decided it was time to dance. So on this blazing hot and humid afternoon, with all the beer bottles and drink glasses sweating on the bar, causing puddles, Charlie climbs up on the bar, walks from the back of the bar to the front of the bar, knocking over six or seven drinks in route, and then starts to dance. First he was dancing slowly - not to the music (Charlie has no rhythm). Then, suddenly, he started dancing wildly – not to the band's music, but to his own drummer. He was dancing on the bar, arms flailing, faster than the music, when he slipped on the wet bar and tumbled. He hit a bar stool as he fell and landed on his face and neck. One woman screamed. The band stopped playing. The place temporarily became silent. People at the bar were stunned - then someone immediately called 911.

Then, while lying on the ground, face slightly scratched and the customers in silence, Charlie hollers out, "Where's the fucking music." Almost on key, the band picks up where they left off, with "Sweet Caroline," and the customers all start laughing at the situation – and singing again. Charlie himself was laughing and crying at the same time. A nurse in the crowd immediately went over after Charlie fell. She said it was a good thing he was drunk or he could have really gotten hurt. The place again erupted in laughter.

The nurse tells Charlie not to move, at all, until the ambulance arrives. Charlie asks the bartender for a Jack Daniels and Coke as he is on the ground, waiting for the ambulance. A bartender gives Charlie the drink he wants. The nurse repeats, "You better not move until the ambulance gets here," thinking Charlie was going to lift his head to consume the drink. Instead, Charlie has a waitress hold the glass next to his mouth as he sips from the bent straw. Then within a few minutes the ambulance arrives. The band stops again as they cart Charlie out. Charlie gives a "thumbs up" as they take him away. The customers cheer him again. The music starts up immediately and the scene is festive.

After Charlie was carted away, the procedure at the bar changed. The bartenders start putting cash from sales into the tip containers, not the register. Familiar customers are buying rounds for other customers and not being charged. It has become a "free for all" behind the bar.

▶ Bart's Assessment:

Obviously, Charlie is a real moron. He sustained a broken collarbone and facial abrasions. He's his own worst nightmare. He's bad for business. By the next summer, Charlie was "long gone."

Chapter 54

You Disgusting Pig!!! (Part 1)

Upon taking a seat at the bar, there were two attractive female patrons at the bar; one with shoulder length dirty blonde hair, and her companion had curly, light brown hair. These female patrons appeared to be friendly with bartender Sonny. At times, they were talking to him as he was preparing drinks. These females were attempting to keep Sonny's attention on them. The two females started kissing each other and laughing, attempting to gain Sonny's attention on multiple occasions when he was busy. At approximately 11:10 P.M., Sonny was talking to these females. He then retrieved a bottle of Maker's Mark from the bar, removed the pourer top, and slid the bottle across the bar to the blonde female. The female then took a "swig" of the Makers Mark from the bottle and handed it back to Sonny. Sonny then screwed the cap on the bottle and placed it back on the shelf.

▶ Bart's Assessment:

Not just would I fire Sonny, but... I think I'd kick his ass on the way out the door. How dare he allow someone to drink from the bottle – and then put the pourer back on!! Eeewww....
He did get fired after the G.M. saw the report.

Chapter 55

Priceless

At 6.43 P.M., a male patron entered and walked up to the end of the bar. He did not take a seat. Bartender Julie walked over to take his drink order. The patron ordered a "Ketel Martini Dirty Up." Julie replied by saying "I'm not making any Martinis until Happy Hour is over" (which was at 7:00 P.M.). She further told the patron, "in the time I make that, I can serve three people" (the bar itself was all but empty at that time). The patron could not believe it. He then said to Julie, "In the time it's taken us to have this conversation, you could have made it! It's vodka with a splash of olive juice - not complicated." Julie then shot back, "Why don't you have something else?" The patron said, "I don't want something else. You're a bartender. It's your job to make drinks." Julie walks away and the patron exited.

▶ Bart's assessment:

Absolutely true and amazing. The patron was right. It is the bartender's job to MAKE DRINKS! A bartender who won't make a certain type of drink can barely be called a bartender. Julie loses a tip, the bar owner loses a sale and a customer. I'd fire the lazy bum that did this to me if I was the owner.

Chapter 56

You Disgusting Pig!!! (Part 2)

Bartender Jake was very busy and it was very hot in the club. Jake was sweating noticeably. While working, Jake was continually touching his sweaty face and hair. He would also rub his eyes, nose and cheeks, as well. He would then prepare drinks (scoop ice) without washing his hands.

▶ Bart's Assessment:

You Disgusting Pig!!!

Chapter 57

I'm Hungry! What's Good?

The only menu present was the electric black board at the entrance to the bar. It listed pulled pork, pulled beef, hot sausage and hot dogs. When the spotter wanted to order a pulled pork sandwich, Joanie looked the spotter in his eyes and shook her head as she mouthed the word "No." The spotter then asked for the pulled beef and received the same response from Joanie. The Hot Sausage was next. Again, he received the same reaction. Then the spotter asked "Hot dog?" Joanie replied, "Great selection!"

After finishing her cigarette, Joanie went in the back room and microwaved a hot dog and served it to the spotter on a stale bun, in a napkin, in a basket. The hot dog was served with packets of mustard and ketchup. The packet of mustard the spotter used had an "off" taste.

▶ Bart's Assessment:

If a kitchen doesn't have at least one "original" type of item on the menu, then why bother? Even if it's hand cut French fries. Something. Anything that tastes good.

What happened here is typical of so many places (and owners). They use cheap, frozen food, which is always lousy. It embarrasses those who serve it. Using the microwave tells you all you need to know about this owner. Microwaved food does not create an influx of patrons. Just the opposite. If the food I ordered was microwaved, I would NEVER return to that place to eat. Microwaving food drives business away. This place is a busy neighborhood bar, but they serve little food. No wonder: Bad mustard? Unheard of! If they would ever improve the quality and originality of the food, and hire a real cook, it could become the "go to" place in the neighborhood. Now, for food, the "locals" go two blocks away to a competing bar that is often busy.

The owner completely disagreed about microwaved food. He said, when cooked properly, microwaved food "is fine." I told him "fine" doesn't cut it when I'm eating. He said we can 'agree to disagree.' Meanwhile, he continues to sell little food.

Chapter 58

You Disgusting Pig!!! (Part 3)

The topic here was Condition of Lavatory:

Horrific. No attendant present. The entire men's room area had a strong, foul odor. There was an explosion of vomit in one of the men's stalls along with urine and fecal matter. The floor had areas of pooling wetness. There were also several napkins on the ground soaked in the matter. The sink area was dirty, wet, and unsanitary.

▶ Bart's Assessment:

I would never go back! And mind you, this report is from a very upscale restaurant.

After the spotter checked this lavatory, his job was over and he exited. Within a half block, he "lost" his meal between two parked cars.

Chapter 59

"I'll Have A Burger" "I'll Have A Burger"

A patron named "Tim" (late 60s, missing teeth) was served a beer by Bartender Bill after he already appeared intoxicated (loud, obnoxious, overbearing, not making sense when speaking, and he was making vulgar comments to female patrons). Tim was apparently a "regular" at the bar. He was tolerated by many of the patrons and staff, but some not familiar with him found him bothersome and obnoxious. He was "forcing" drunken conversations with patrons ('hitting' on females while using vulgar language). At 11:30 P.M., Tim ordered a burger from the waitress. When the waitress went to place the order for the burger, Tim ordered another burger from the bartender Bill. Approximately 8 minutes later, the waitress served the burger to him. Three minutes later, the bartender served a burger to him. At that point, Tim told the bartender that he ordered from the waitress. This resulted in the waitress telling drunken Tim that he is not supposed to order the same food from two different employees. Tim did not accept the second burger. He then complained that the burger he was eating was overcooked.

▶ Bart's Assessment:

Tim should have been "cutoff" long before this incident occurred. He was clearly drunk and offensive towards patrons. The owner immediately put a rule in place for future, similar incidents. He told the staff that if the patron looks even slightly drunk, *"DO NOT SERVE THEM."* Instead, the owner said to call a cab for them and attempt to get them out of the bar as quickly as possible. Avoid calling police. Excellent advice!

Chapter 60

Tipping Out

A t 12:39 A.M., There was a conversation between bartender George and the barback that was loud enough for the spotter and others at the bar to overhear clearly. The barback was taking empty beer pitchers from George as they began to talk about work schedules and "tipping procedures" for the employees. George made the comment, "I did not know that. It's funny how I am always the last to know," and "I already have to split tips three ways as it is.... And you're saying I have to give 20% more on top of that."

► **Bart's Assessment:**

Anytime an employee mentions the "T" word in front of patrons, it sounds like they are begging for tips. No matter what the context may be. In this instance, it was none of the patrons business to hear this.

Chapter 61

Irresponsible – Say Bye Bye Liquor License

A female patron who appeared to be 20 – 21 years old sat at a table away from the bar. She was with a male patron who appeared to be close to 40 years old. The male stepped up to the bar and ordered two drinks, one Martini and a Jack Daniels/Coke. After paying, he returned to the table with the two drinks. The female consumed the Martini and the male had the Jack/Coke. The female was not carded.

▶ Bart's Assessment:

Seriously, any bartender who does not card patrons of that age should be fired, immediately!!! Carding patrons is in their job description.

Chapter 62

The Dreaded Buyback

1:45 A.M., A male patron seated near spotter orders Blue Point lager. As he starts to pay for the beer, the bartender says to him, "I'll get this round; it's your fourth, time for the buyback." This buyback was not accounted for via they register, after service (no "comp" sheet updated at that time).

► Bart's Assessment:

I love when bartenders say "I'll get this round." Bartenders never "get a round" of anything. It's always the owner!

But regarding the buyback. It was supposedly the patron's fourth beer. The spotter thought it was the patron's third. Very arbitrary. The question here: Is this practice really necessary? Aside from the cost, four drinks for the price of three, the sobriety of those patrons comes into question. Also, can the bartender really remember which drink is the patron's fourth if the bar becomes busy? Many bar owners offer the fourth drink "buyback." The question is: Why? It would be better for business if the owner stopped in, every now and then, and 'bought' a round for the house. It works wonders for business and bartender tips!

Chapter 63

"Hey, I'm Busy, Don't Bother Me"

Bartender Marcy had two groups of male patrons that she was focused on. She would lean on the bar and chat with them often, during the visit. On those occasions, she was not looking around the bar for patrons in need of service (many patrons required service). Patrons would have to walk over to that area and wave or call to her, for drink service. Marcy served approximately 15% - 20% of the drinks at the bar during this time. The other 2 bartenders served the other 80% - 85% of the drinks.

▶ Bart's Assessment:

The owners of the bar responded exactly as they should have. They fired Marcy at the end of the shift, before the tips were counted. There was $270 in the tips that night. They gave Marcy $20 of that cash before throwing her ass out!!! The other bartenders, who served most of the drinks, divided the remainder of the tips.

Chapter 64

Let's Sit Here! No Here! No Here!

Bartender Josh commented (loud enough for the spotter to hear), regarding the seating of a group of six patrons at tables near the bar. Josh said, "Where do they get off sitting at a table near the bar - and not at the bar! Fuck! I have ten empty seats at my bar and they sit at a table!" Josh then mocked the patrons by saying "Oh, we want to sit at a table..." Josh then said, "Fuck you! Sit at the bar.... Now I have to walk all the way around!"

► Bart's Assessment:

What just happened here? Did this lazy, inept bartender Josh say that he didn't want to walk over to a table to serve patrons? In reality, the table was approximately ten feet away and the bar was not busy. Then, Josh used profanity as he mocked the customers, aloud.

Remember, customers are the guests of the owner when they are in the bar. Without customers, no bar!

The owner agreed with me. Josh does not have to walk over to tables at this place anymore. He now receives unemployment checks from the State of NJ.

Chapter 65

Bartender Who Sit On Cooler Get 'Behind' In Work

Bartender Jamie spent approximately 80% of this time in deep conversation with a male patron who was seated in the corner of the bar closest to the restroom. She would lean on the bar, as well as place a small towel on the beer cooler and sit on the cooler to be close to him. This male consumed sodas and was not charged. Other patrons at the bar had empty drink containers and were not offered refills in a timely manner.

▶ Bart's Assessment:

I know a perfect place for a bartender who ignores patrons to conduct "lovey dovey" conversations while on duty. It's the Unemployment Office (if there is still an office). This bartender is hurtful towards business. This conduct should not have to be tolerated by any owner of any business.

Chapter 66

Fumble!!!

10:46 P.M. – Bartender Chris withdraws cash from his pocket and he fumbles with it for a few seconds. He then walks over to a large sized male patron he had been in conversation with. Chris then handed the cash across the bar to him. The spotter could not determine what that cash represented. The patron placed that cash in his shirt pocket.

▶ Bart's assessment:

If the owner was on the other side of the room observing this, or watching on surveillance camera, what would he think? Here is what should go through the owner's head:

Was that cash, handed across the bar, from his pocket?

Why was that cash handed across the bar?

Was that cash from the register, from sales?

Was that cash for drugs?

Was that cash for gambling?

Was that cash for food delivery?

Whenever a bartender reaches into his pants pocket and then does anything with cash, it has "the look of impropriety." That owner MUST get to the bottom of this situation quickly, or else he risks losing his business.

Chapter 67

Baby The Rain Must Fall

A pool league, consisting of 16 players and many onlookers were ready for their 10:00 P.M. start. At 9:50 P.M., the bouncer informed bartender Mike that they were "closing" the pool table due to a hole in the roof that was allowing the rain to fall on the pool table. The bouncer said he was putting a bucket on the table.

▶ Bart's Assessment:

Get it fixed! This is TERRIBLE for business.

Chapter 68

Warm Beer Anyone?

The center door on the reach-in beer cooler was left open from 9:18 P.M. - 9:47 P.M. Both bartenders walked past the open door of the cooler on multiple occasions and neither closed it. Finally, a patron reached across the bar and closed it.

► Bart's Assessment:

If the bartenders want to drive away business, this is a 'sure fire' method. NOBODY likes warm beer. The fact that 2 bartenders were on duty, and neither of them took the time to close the door to the reach-in is shameful and disrespectful to the owner and patrons. The owner didn't like it either. He suspended both bartenders due to this, and both quit him. Owner wins this one.

Chapter 69

Copping A Smoke

At 10:50 P.M., bartender Eli went outside for a smoke. At that time, there was male patron seated at the bar with an empty drink glass, waiting for a replacement drink. Eli returned behind the bar at 10:57 P.M. On this occasion, the waitress was not covering the bar during Eli's absence. The patron exited before Eli returned and the sale was lost.

► Bart's Assessment:

Losing business for the bar to go outside to smoke. That's bad, but it's not the real crime here. The real crime is that Eli did not have someone (like the waitress) watch the bar during his absence. The owner's response – Eli was suspended for one night – a Saturday (this place's busiest night of the week).

Chapter 70

Waiting For Nate "Wanna Get High"

At approximately 12:25 A.M., a male patron named Nate, wearing a baseball cap backwards, exited the bar twice within 30 minutes to go to the bathroom. He mentioned to spotter's companion that he was on a date with the girl with dark brown hair who was sitting to the right. Then when the spotter was about to exit at 2:00 A.M., Nate was gone from his earlier seat next to the female with long brown hair. She was still in her original seat on mid left side of bar, not far from door. She was overheard by the companion saying to another patron, 'So you're waiting for Nate, trying to get high, too?'

▶ Bart's Assessment:

This happens too much anymore. Drug dealers in bars. Circulating among the clientele, competing with the bar owner for the patron's dollar. If a patron at the bar spends $10 with the "pusher" (a dime bag), that's $10 he won't spend on drinks. It could become costly. Bar owners should really consider this: You will lose your liquor license if this "pusher" gets caught 'dealing' in your place. Plain and simple. A strong manager could easily prevent this from happening. DON'T let it happen to you!!!

Chapter 71

Reflections...

A former strip club owner, aptly named Connie Cox, calls Bart and told him she needs a spotter for a specific night. After ten years in the strip club business and not making any money, Connie decided she wanted to make her place a neighborhood bar. She explained to Bart, "the transition from Strip Club to neighborhood bar has been tough." The Strip Club patrons stopped coming. And the "word" in the area, that it was a neighborhood bar, was slow to spread." Bart asked Connie what the spotters could do for her, if the volume of business was THAT low. She said to him, "well, that's the point. Little cash in the register, yet my liquor costs are way more than they should be. Maybe you guys can help me figure it out."

The next night Bart entered a bit after midnight. There were two other customers at the bar, a guy and a girl and they left fifteen minutes later. There was the bartender named Tabitha and a guy who Bart thought was an employee, but when he was given a drink by Tabitha, a Jack Daniels/Coke prepared with an excessive amount of Jack, it made Bart think he was a friend, not an employee (to cut to the chase, it turned out that he was Tabitha's boyfriend). A few minutes after Tabitha gave him the drink, she prepared a drink for herself, a Captain Morgan's/Coke, also prepared with an excessive amount of liquor. This helps to explain why Connie's liquor costs were so high. Liquor going out and no cash coming in.

So Bart was sitting there, and after a bit of time, he was the only "patron" at the bar. He made like he was watching TV, but he was really watching them. Tabitha and the boyfriend were at the other end of the bar drinking and laughing. Nothing else going on.

Bart's beer was running low. Tabitha walked over and asked if he wanted another. He accepted the offer. Tabitha served the beer and accounted for it. She then told Bart that she had "some things to do" and she would be "in the back." She then told him she would check back with him soon.

Tabitha then returns to the other end of the bar with the boyfriend. Both were there drinking and talking for the next few minutes. Then Tabitha walked on the stage, towards the back room. As she walked, there was a series of mirrors that remained from the days when the club was a strip club. Bart followed Tabitha in the mirrors, then momentarily lost sight of her.

A couple of minutes have passed and the boyfriend is sipping his drink at the bar. He then left his drink on the bar, got up from his seat and walked towards the back. He followed Tabitha's same path, walking on the stage, along the mirrored wall, and then momentarily out of sight.

With Bart alone at the bar and no one else around, he moved down a seat to see if he could see Tabitha or the boyfriend in the back, through the mirrors.

Looking along the mirrored wall, Bart saw some movement in the very last mirror. It was a partial view of the boyfriend and it looked like he was just leaning against the wall. Tabitha was not in sight. Probably working.

"Something must be going on here," Bart thought, but he had no idea of what was happening.

The boyfriend was still there, partially obscured in the mirror, seemingly doing nothing.

Bart then moves down another seat or two to have a better view. At this point, two newly arriving customers, both males, take seats at the bar, only a few seats away. After a two minute wait, they asked

Bart if there was a bartender working. Bart tells them that she was "in the back with her boyfriend." The two customers started laughing. They joked, "What is she doing back there, sucking his dick?"

Bart then told them that he could see the boyfriend in the mirror, but he hasn't seen the bartender for a few minutes. The two guys then move towards Bart, so they can also see the boyfriend in the mirror. As soon as the two new guys moved next to Bart, he showed them the boyfriend in the mirror. Then, almost on cue, Tabitha's head lifts up. Indeed, she was "performing the deed." The spotter and the two guys had moved into a perfect position where they all had a great view. The two guys went wild. They were loving it. A free sex show right there in Connie Cox's. Both guys said it was better than when it was a Strip Club!

Bart continues, "So now, Tabitha must come out from the back room and serve the patrons. It should be interesting. These two guys were laughing hysterically."

A couple of minutes have passed since the sex show in the mirrors. The boyfriend returned to his drink, but won't make eye contact with Bart or the 2 guys, who now really want a drink. Within the next minute, Tabitha returned behind the bar. Bart and the two guys at the bar are doing all they could to refrain from laughing. One of the guys, in a kidding manner told Tabitha, "we thought you got lost." He then asked Tabitha, also in a joking way, "where were you?" Tabitha replied, "busy doing things." He said, "we need drinks." They ordered two beers. As Tabitha walks away to retrieve the beers, one of the guys says, "yeah, doing him" (pointing at the boyfriend).

Bart Assessment:

This gave a new meaning to "downtime."

Chapter 72

Managing What?

Manager Diane "covered" the bar during the bartender's ten minute absence. During her time behind the bar, Diane prepared a couple of drinks for the Service window. She then prepared a drink for herself in a pint glass consisting of one third ice, one third glass of Stoli O, and a clear mixer. After the bartender returned behind the bar, Diane took the drink, walked around to a seat at the bar, and sat there, and consumed it.

▶ Bart's Assessment:

Very bad! Very very bad!! Any manager that consumes a drink in front of staff, at ANY time, is committing a No-No. There is a time and place for everything – except this! The manager is on duty to 'watch' the liquor, not drink it. When the owner got wind of this occurrence, he fired her immediately. Too many "what ifs."

Chapter 73

Hat's Off To Roxy

At 9:49 P.M., bartender Roxy "sold" a baseball style hat (with the bar logo) to a male patron at the bar. Roxy appeared familiar with this male. She tossed the hat at him and ten seconds later he acknowledged he wanted it. She used the register as a calculator to tell him the price was $17, but did not ring the sale through the register. Then, immediately after, Roxy prepared two "tall Jack/ Cokes" for two different patrons, containing two shots of Jack in each, for a total of $18. The sale of the mixed drinks was transacted on the screen by clearing the $17 Hat screen and ringing the drink sale for $18. Therefore, the sale of the hat was not completed.

► Bart's Assessment:

The patron got the hat for free. When the owner read the report, he did not seem to mind. He said it would advertise the bar when the guy wore it. That's partially true. It would "advertise" the bar. But to what extent might it help? Probably little to none.

The correct thing for the bartender to have done was to let the owner know, in some way, that she gave away that hat. Instead, he read it in the spotter report. He was not amused. Ultimately, he would rather have the $17 in the register. Can't blame him. It's his hat!!

Chapter 74

That's Using The Register!

At 12:10 A.M., bartender Steve received a food delivery. He had cash in his hand to pay the delivery person. However, he did not have enough cash in hand for a tip. Steve told the delivery person to "wait a second." At that point, Steve rang the register, withdrew $3, and gave it to the delivery person as a tip.

▶ Bart's Assessment:

$3 tip. No big deal. Right?

Wrong! I had real trouble believing this and so did the owner. Instead of taking the $3 from his tip container, which had lots of cash in it, he chose to ring the register and take $3 from there. It's thievery any way you look at it!

The owner of this place took offense to Steve using the register for his food delivery tip. He suspended Steve for a weekend, which prompted Steve to quit. The owner was the big winner here.

Chapter 75

Can't You See I'm On The Phone???

The question on the report reads: Is Bartender Offering Prompt Drink Service? The answer was: Not at all.…

11:05 P.M., A male patron entered and took a seat at the bar next to the spotter, who was seated mid-bar. Bartender Tabitha was standing directly across from the spotter talking on her cell phone. When the male took a seat next to the spotter, Tabitha held up one finger, as if to say she would be right with him.

11:09 P.M., The spotter's drink is now empty and there are other empty drink containers on the bar, with patrons waiting for replacement service. Tabitha is still on the phone, leaning on the back bar, facing the patrons who were waiting – but looking downward. She has not served any patrons in the last 7 or 8 minutes. The patron who took a seat next to the spotter exited (he said to the spotter, "what da fuck, can't get a drink here!").

▶ Bart's Assessment:

We would be remiss in our reporting if we did not mention cell phones. This type of activity is commonplace anymore. An employee texting, or making a call, or receiving a call occurs almost every shift. But it shouldn't. In fact, cell phones

should be banned from usage if a bartender is on duty. If they have an emergency, then call on the land line or wait until they get a break. Otherwise, "hey, you're at work, hang up the phone and serve the customers."

Chapter 76

But With Employees Like This – It Could Be Fun

Both bartenders on duty during this time followed the same procedure when accounting for drinks. Cash or tab update, every sale was accounted for immediately after service. Change was returned and patrons were thanked for their purchases and tips. For tabs, the bartenders are informing there is a $20 minimum for credit card usage.

▶ Bart's Assessment:

Yes!!! There are plenty of good and honest bartenders out there. The trick of this business is to find them and keep them happy.

In Conclusion

I think everybody gets the drift by now. Consider *"Bar Scam's Exposed!"* as a learning experience for all. Bartenders can use this guide for misdirection, and the bar owners can use it to stop that "misdirection." Either way, winners all!!

▶ Bart's Final Assessment:

Bar patrons seeking entertainment at the bar SHOULD read this guide!

Bartenders MUST read this guide!

Bar owners BETTER read this guide!

And Just One More Thing

We would LOVE to hear your best (true) bar stories. The stories could involve love, drinking, bartenders, food, music, DJs, Barmaids, drugs, fights, or whatever. Send your best stories the E-Mail address:

barscamsexposed@gmail.com

Made in the USA
Coppell, TX
03 June 2022

78437583R10105